Montague R. Leverson

Common Sense

First steps in political economy, for the use of families and normal classes, and of

pupils in district, elementary and grammar schools - being a popular introduction to

the most important truths regarding labor and capital

Montague R. Leverson

Common Sense
First steps in political economy, for the use of families and normal classes, and of pupils in district, elementary and grammar schools - being a popular introduction to the most important truths regarding labor and capital

ISBN/EAN: 9783337239244

Printed in Europe, USA, Canada, Australia, Japan

Cover: Foto ©Suzi / pixelio.de

More available books at **www.hansebooks.com**

COMMON SENSE;

OR,

First Steps in Political Economy,

FOR THE USE OF

FAMILIES AND NORMAL CLASSES,

AND OF

Pupils in District, Elementary and Grammar Schools;

Being a Popular Introduction to

THE MOST IMPORTANT TRUTHS REGARDING
LABOR AND CAPITAL.

BY

M! R. LEVERSON, Dr. Ph., M. A.,

Attorney-at-Law,

Author of "Copyright and Patents, or Property in Thought," "The
Natural History of a Cause, according to English and English-
derived Procedure;" "The Rational System of Legal
Procedure," "Rational Schools," "The Uses
and Functions of Money;" "The American
System of Education," "Draft of a
Constitution for Colorado,"
etc., etc.

NEW YORK:
THE AUTHORS' PUBLISHING COMPANY.
CHAIN & HARDY: Denver, Col.
1876.

PREFACE.

THIS work is published, chiefly, in the hope of its having some influence towards the introduction of the teaching of moral and economical science in our schools. It is also intended to help all persons, including children, even without the aid of a teacher, to acquire some knowledge of the most important truths of those sciences.

It will, it is hoped, be impossible for any person, after reading this little work, to question the practicability of imparting a competent knowledge of morals and of political economy even to young children. The circumstances which gave occasion to the work furnish additional evidence of this fact.

In the winter of 1867-8 the author, as a volunteer teacher, gave a series of lessons in the Saturday Normal School of New York to a class of post-graduate teachers "on the object and method of imparting to young children a knowledge of the conditions of human well-being, commonly called 'political economy'." The class numbered about thirty at its commencement, and about thirty-five at its close, and, although the teachers could gain no advancement whatever from their attendance, their punctuality was remarkable, and equalled, if it did not exceed, that of any other class in the institution, although attendance at such other classes on the part of the under-graduate teachers was indispensable to their advancement. The teachers who attended the author's lessons became enthusiastic for the introduction of the teaching of the science into our schools, while the effect upon their own minds, in the additional power it gave them in their teaching was such, that nearly every member of that class has become noted as a specially skilled and earnest teacher. But, although there was patent the certainly unusual fact of a gentleman, unconnected with the schools, giving his time to further the cause of good education, of a number of post graduate teachers regularly giving up their one holiday a week for the sake of benefitting by his labors, not a single School Commissioner or Trustee of the city of New York ever put foot inside the class-room, which, nevertheless, was regularly attended by one of New York's most respected merchants!

Repeatedly, in the course of the lessons, the teachers asked the author to recommend them text-books, to enable them to pursue further the studies to which he introduced them, and particularly for use in schools.

Beyond referring them to standard works upon Economic Science, there were none to which the author could refer as specially adapted for either purpose. Admirable as are the works of Mr. Wm. Ellis, and great as has been the author's use of Mr. Ellis's teachings, these works are not appropriate for use in our schools, and, at the earnest request of those teachers, the author wrote a book on political economy, which he hopes may serve as an introductory text-book.

In the suggestions which are given to teachers some hints will be found as to the use to be made of this book. The author desires, however, to insist especially on the truth that the most efficient part of all teaching is the ORAL; and he urges on teachers to fit themselves to give that kind of teaching, using this work as a text-book for THEMSELVES even more than for their pupils; but, also employing this work AS A READING BOOK, carefully seeing that the pupils understand each sentence before proceeding to another. The great attention paid in nearly all our schools to the study of grammar will render this task comparatively easy, while the practical application of the lessons in grammar studied by the pupils, to the perusal and study of a work on a different science, will serve to give them an interest in their grammatical lessons, which the judicious teacher will know how to utilize.

This work was written under circumstances when the author was almost without resources in the way of referring to authorities. He has referred in all cases, in the text, to the authorities he has quoted, except in the case of quoting from the works of

Mr. Wm. Ellis. Strange as it may seem, it is yet a fact that, though the author is conscious of having repeatedly availed himself of Mr. Ellis's ideas, and often even of his language, he is unable to refer any quotation to its proper work, or place in that work.

When writing this book, the author had none of Mr. Ellis's works at hand for reference, nothing but a rather copious abstract of those works made many years before. In many cases his quotations are unconscious, in all, as imperfect as might be expected from their being made from memory, aided only by such abstract.

Much of what the author has learned of political economy—all that he learned, otherwise than by experience, of the method of teaching it—he learned from Mr. Wm. Ellis and from Mr. Shields, one of the ablest of Mr. Ellis's disciples, but chiefly in converse with them—*that is, orally.* Whenever, then, any coincidence of ideas or language between this book and any of Mr. Ellis's may be found, to Mr. Ellis and not to the author belongs the merit of originality; nevertheless, in most cases, the author's use of such ideas will have been derived from Mr. Ellis's conversation and oral teachings, (which, in the author's case, generally preceded the publication by Mr. Ellis of his works,) his books having been developed by Mr. Ellis out of his oral discussions with his numerous disciples, while his ideas and language imparted to, and in many cases assimilated by his disciples, have been afterwards given to the world in his published writings.

Under these circumstances, reference on each occasion to the particular work in which any idea might be found became impossible, and this general acknowledgement the more necessary.

The author has also to acknowledge his indebtedness to Mr. Charles Moran, and specially to Mr. Richard L. Dugdale, both of New York, for their kindness in revising the manuscript, and for many most valuable criticisms and suggestions.

Essential as it is that our future legislators should not be allowed to grow up ignorant of the important truths of economic science, it is the moral teachings of the science which the author regards as of the greatest moment.

The opponents of our public schools are right in urging the deplorable absence of moral teaching and training, so "conspicuous by their absence" from the curriculum, as an objection and a fatal objection to the existing system. Even as the economic blunders of Congress are the logical consequences of the absence of all teaching of economic science from our common schools, in which schools its members were mostly reared, and which are the nurseries of our future statesmen, even so the moral obliquity of citizens and officials, the worship of success without regard to the means by which it has been obtained, the corruption and untrustworthiness which are rife among us, are the results of the absence of moral teaching and training from those same schools in which the merchant and official have been trained.

To remove the evil the cause must be removed. Let the future generation of statesmen and of citizens receive in childhood that teaching and training by which alone they can be preserved from like errors; and when they grow up they will not only avoid those errors themselves, but correct those of their predecessors.

But how shall this instruction be provided for the future citizen when our teachers themselves are ignorant alike of the science and of the method of teaching it? The answer is obvious. Introduce the teaching of the science and of the method of teaching it into the NORMAL SCHOOLS.

Nowhere in any normal school on this broad continent, so far as the author has been able to learn, is any such instruction being imparted to the future teachers of our youth as we now see to be so necessary ; yet the teachers are ready to be taught, as the author's experiment in 1867-8 testifies, and as the following fact will serve further to demonstrate :

The author attended the meeting of the Teachers' Association, held at Boston some years ago, and availed himself of the discussion following the reading of a paper in one of the sections, to introduce the subject of teaching political economy to the young. When his ten minutes had expired, by the unanimous vote of the meeting the entire residue of the time appointed for discussion on the paper which had given the pretext for his observations, was given to the author ; and at its termination the discussion was continued to a free hour, at the close of which one of the teachers, in the name of himself and all the teachers present, and amid their enthusiastic acclamations, declared the discussion thus rather irregularly introduced to have been more profitable than all that had theretofore taken place at the meeting of the Association, and asked the author to appoint a day, in the daytime or evening, after the association exercises should be closed, to resume the subject. To his own great regret, he was unable to comply with the request, the calls of business having necessitated his leaving Boston before the close of the meeting.

The teachers, then, are ready, but they are obliged to wait upon those to whose care our educational interests are confided, and these last are hardly likely to make the required move until urged on by outside pressure. Let press and people, then, join in the cry, REFORM THE NORMAL SCHOOLS, and thus make our Centennial "fruitful in good works."

DENVER, COLORADO, July 4th, 1876.

** *Review Questions* and some suggestions to help *teachers* and *self-students* will be found in the *Appendix* at end of the work.

1*

CONTENTS.

(11)

CHAPTER XI.

CHAPTER XVII.

CHAPTER XVIII.

CHAPTER XIX.

CHAPTER XX.

APPENDIX.

First Steps in Political Economy.

CHAPTER I.

COMFORTS SURROUNDING CHILDREN IN THE UNITED STATES. HOW PROCURED. HISTORY OF A STOCKING. IDEA AND NAME OF WEALTH. IMPORTANCE OF THE CORRECT USE OF WORDS TO EXPRESS IDEAS.

1. The comforts of children in the United States.—The children of this favored land rise every morning from a comfortable bed to find clothing ready for them to put on, water, (perhaps brought from a great distance,) for their use, soap, towel, comb and brush, all ready to their hands.

Having washed and dressed, they help, if old enough and in good health, in kindling the fires and sweeping and cleaning the rooms and furniture, they brush their boots and shoes, and help to make ready the breakfast for the family.

Having breakfasted, they gather their books together and go to school. There they find a school-room, generally well warmed, supplied with fresh, pure air, and fitted with desks, maps, charts, slates and many other things to add to their comfort, or to help them in gaining knowledge, while a kind and earnest teacher is waiting to show them the hard places, and make their lessons plain and easy.

The school session over, the children return home to a loving father and mother, who are happy when their children are happy, and are always ready to try to save them from trouble or harm.

At home they again find food ready for them, and after learning a few easy lessons for the morrow, and spending some time in playing with dolls or balls, bats, tops or skates, they bathe in a tub of water, hot or cold, as may be best for their health or cleanliness, and go to bed without any fear lest any one of the comforts enjoyed to-day should be wanting to them to-morrow.

2. Children have become so used to all these comforts and enjoyments that they do not think how much time has been spent, and how much *labor* done, not only by their parents, but by many other persons also, in order to get these things for them, and they give little thought to the difficulties which had to be overcome to bring many of the things they use from different parts of the world.

3. Let us take up one of the articles in common use among children, say a pair of woolen stockings, and trace its history from its beginning until it is brought to them for use. Let us also see what kind of men and women they must be by whom the stocking is produced and supplied to the children.

4. *History of a Stocking.*—The wool of which the stocking is woven was grown on the backs of sheep, raised with much care and labor, perhaps in Ohio or Iowa, Texas, New Mexico, Colorado or California, or possibly in Australia or the Cape of Good Hope. Sheared in due season, it has been transported in cars, drawn by steam locomotives, or carried in ships, (the building of which had occupied many men for many months,) to the ports of New York, Boston or Liverpool; where depots, piers, docks and warehouses had been laboriously constructed for the reception of the cars and ships and for the storage of the wool, until the manufacturer was ready to receive it.

5. To the manufacturer the wool was carried over a road which crosses broad and deep rivers, spans valleys, bores through mountains, and costs in building the labor of many times more men for many times more months than did the building of the ship.

6. Having reached the factory, the changes the wool has to undergo to fit it as a covering for the feet may now be said to commence.

7. First it is picked and cleaned, then carded in a machine which was produced by great labor on the part of many laborers, driven by an engine, also *the product of much labor and skill*, while fuel has been dug out of the earth or cut down from forests, and laboriously transported to the engine, in order that this latter may drive the carding machine.

8. The wool is then spun on a spinning machine, driven by an engine which is fed by fuel, *all the products of. great labor and skill.*

9. The wool is now converted into a thread to which the name of yarn is given, and this yarn is next dyed and then woven on a loom or knitted into a stocking.

10. The stocking is now transported to the warehouse of the wholesale dealer, and by him distributed over the country amongst the storekeepers, so that these may have at hand a supply to meet the demand of the parents of the children by whom the stockings are to be worn.

11. In a like manner may be traced the history of all other articles of clothing; pants, shirts, drawers, dresses, jackets, boots, shoes and hats.

12. So, too, all articles of food ; milk, bread, meat, tea, coffee, sugar, spices and condiments, may in a like manner be traced from the commencement of the labor of their production until they appear upon the table.

13. Products of Labor.—It will be seen that none of them can be produced *except by the expenditure of vast amounts of labor.*

Houses for shelter, school houses as places of instruction, factories for the manufacture of tools, machinery, clothing and furniture, graneries and warehouses for storage, roads and railroads, canals, cars and ships, for the distribution of commodities among manufacturers, traders and consumers, as well as the stores in which they are kept until needed to be eaten, worn or used, all cost great labor for their construction and maintenance.

All these things above enumerated, and many besides, which we call the necessaries and comforts of life, ARE PRODUCED BY LABOR, and can only be so produced.

14. Wealth.—We have now acquired an important thought, viz.: that the necessaries and comforts of life are produced by labor, and to the things thus produced the name of WEALTH has been given.

15. It is essential to the right understanding of any subject that the learner should have a clear and definite notion of the meaning of the language employed in its discussion.

16. This necessity is nowhere greater than in the study of the conditions of human well being; let the pupil therefore clearly understand that by the term wealth is meant the necessaries and comforts of life produced by labor, and that to the idea of the necessaries and comforts of life produced by labor the name wealth and no other will be applied.

17. We shall find by and bye that wealth exists under different conditions, or is applied to various uses; we shall hereafter analyze wealth, *i. e.*, divide it into its component parts, and we shall give a special name to any portion of wealth of which we may need to speak without including any other.

CHAPTER II.

Some necessaries not produced by labor and not included in the term wealth. Earth, air, water, when they are not, and when they are wealth. Production; what it is. Labor creates nothing. It changes the position of matter. We live on the products of past labor. Ideas of economy. Skill and knowledge evolved, and names given.

18. Some necessaries not wealth.—We have seen that most of the necessaries and comforts of life are produced by labor, to these the name of WEALTH has been applied; but there are some necessaries which are not produced by labor; such are the earth, air and water.

19. But, although the earth, air and water, in their natural places and conditions, do not come within our definition of wealth, (for, though necessaries of life, they are not produced by labor,) there are circumstances under which they come within our definition.

20. In coal mines, in the diving-bell, in tne ariving of tunnels, fresh air is supplied to the miner, to the diver and to the excavator, at the cost of considerable labor, and the cost of supplying it in these cases enters largely into the cost of producing

the coal, building the pier, dock or bridge, and in cutting the tunnel.

The water we need for drinking, cleansing, cooking, or other purposes, is generally brought with no little labor to the place where we use it.

The earth must be cultivated and improved before it will give its fruits in abundance. In all these cases air, water and earth are wealth, because they are produced in the place where, or in the condition in which they are required by *labor*.

21. The justice of including these within our definition will become manifest when we examine a little closely what man's labor really does towards the production of food, clothing, fuel, shelter, and other articles of use or enjoyment.

22. What labor does.—LABOR CREATES NOTHING. It can only change the relative positions of particles of matter.

In ploughing, man breaks up the soil and exposes it to the action of the air. To manure it he transports matter containing fertilizing particles from a place where these particles are in excess, and spreads the matter upon his field where they are deficient. He sows the seed—that is, he deposits another form of matter in the ground thus improved, and if he has ploughed and manured his field, and selected and sown the seed with due regard to climate, soil, and nature of the plant, and continues diligently to weed, and, where necessary, to irrigate his land, he has reason, from past experience, to expect to garner a bounteous harvest.

The corn, wheat, or other grain which is the product of the labor of the farmer, is ground into meal or flour, and then made into bread by mixing with it, salt, water and yeast kneaded together, and baked in an oven. No new or additional element or atom of matter is brought into existence, but, by a change in the relative positions of particles of matter, a combination is produced to which the name bread is given; and which, in this new form, is well adapted to satisfy man's needs.

In the process of spinning, weaving, knitting, dyeing, cutting and fitting, building, mining and forging, nothing is created; the positions of particles of matter are shifted, and this is all.

23. When this new arrangement of matter tends to satisfy some want, a *commodity* is produced by labor; and this commodity therefore belongs to that class of things to which the general name WEALTH has been given.

24. The character of the people by whom existing wealth has been produced. — The

people by whom the wealth we now find in existence
was produced must, we see, have been a hard-
working people. The old, the infirm, and young
children are incapable of labor. Their means of
subsistance must be provided for them by those
who can and do labor. The smaller the number of
those who live upon the labor of others, the greater
will be the amount of the necessaries and comforts
of life produced for the enjoyment of all. So also
will the means for such enjoyment increase with the
ability and willingness of those who do labor.

25. This ability and willingness can be acquired
by the young by earnest attention to their school
duties, and by cheerfully assisting their parents in
household or other tasks adapted to their strength.

26. Industry.—To those who labor cheerfully
and continuously in the production of wealth, or in
fitting themselves to become producers, the term
" industrious " is applied, and the quality they possess is termed " INDUSTRY."

27. The quality of industry must have belonged in a
high degree to the men and women of the past,
since we now enjoy so much wealth which they had
accumulated and provided for our use. Children
who think of this will readily learn to love and
practice industry, in order that, when they shall be

grown up to be men and women, and take part in
the business of production, they may cheerfully,
willingly and continuously labor to replace the
stores consumed by them in infancy and childhood,
to provide for their then present and-future wants,
as well as to bear their share of the burthen of sup-
porting those who shall have succeeded to their
places in the ranks of non-workers.

28. In passing in review the manner in which are
produced some of the commodities in common use,
the question must have suggested itself to the mind
of the thoughtful student—what were men living upon
while digging and ploughing, sowing and reaping,
rearing cattle, building, spinning, baking and the
like?

29. We live on the products of past labor.
—The wealth which man's labor is engaged in producing cannot be employed to satisfy his present
needs, the results of that labor do not exist in the
present, but are expected to exist at some future
time. Evidently, then, *man lives on the products of
his labor in the past*, the saving of which for future
consumption was a necessity soon forced upon his
notice.

30. In nothing is the contrast more distinctly
marked between the savage and the civilized man,

2

than in the forethought which renders it part of the present enjoyment of the latter to provide for the *future* wants of himself and family. Thus, the very act of abstaining from the complete gratification of his and their present needs, in order that their future wants may be supplied, forms a part of the happiness of the civilized man ; while nothing could cause him greater mental suffering, than to be compelled to consume all his present store, with the prospect of being unable to obtain a future supply.

31. The savage, on the contrary, cannot be induced to abstain from wasting what he cannot immediately enjoy, however terrible may have been the sufferings of himself and family through past wastefulness.

32. Saving.—The necessity of saving will be, perhaps, more vividly realized by the young by noting the following facts :

33. In most countries there is but one principal harvest in the year ; but man's need for food occurs three or four times every day, neither Sundays nor holidays being excepted. How, then, can he make one harvest gratify the cravings of three times three hundred and sixty-five appetites, but by saving? But, further, harvests sometimes fail, or are late, or deficient, and the abundance of one year must,

therefore, be stored up to supply the failure, lateness, or deficiency of the next. Savages are incapable of looking so far forward into the future, and hence their tribes are being continually decimated by famine and its sure successors pestilence and disease.

34. It is impossible fully to appreciate the very large amount of saving from the products of past labor which must have been practised by those who have lived before us, in order that we might procure merely the common things in use in the abundance in which we have them.

35. Among other things it is to be observed that the aqueducts which bring water to our houses—the ships, docks, piers, canals, railroads, wagons and steam cars employed in the transportation of commodities ; the machinery employed in the conversion of raw products into articles of utility—could never have had existence but for such saving. *Their very cost measures, and is measured, by the quantity of saving from the products of previous labor consumed in their construction.*

36. Economy.—The name "economy" is applied to the quality of saving, and this quality we now see must have largely prevailed among parents in order that the children of to-day might enjoy the large supply of comfort provided for them.

37. High among the industrial virtues must the quality of economy be ranked, and its prevalence must be classed as one of the most important conditions of human well-being.

38. The habit of saving once acquired, its practice becomes part of the enjoyment of the present; and when youth shall be generally taught to perceive its importance, a vast increase in the wellbeing of future generations may be confidently predicted.

39. The industry and economy we have seen practised in the past, and which it is desirable should to a yet greater degree be practised in the future, would have availed little to produce an abundance of wealth, if man's faculties were incapable of improvement, or if the ease with which he performs his labor, and the character of its results, were not increased and improved by each repetition ; or if he were unable to store up and record his observations for future use.

40. Skill.—The faculty of performing any certain labor with ease, and of giving an improved character to the results of that labor, is termed " Skill."

51. Knowledge.—To have or possess stored up in the mind, ready for use, observations of past facts,

and the records of past experience, is termed—
" KNOWLEDGE."

42. Skill and knowledge are also needed to observe and record facts, and a knowledge of those facts and of their mutual relations is needed to discover the laws of their modes of action. From observations of these facts and modes of action, the principle of the rotation of crops, the nature, qualities and application of manures, the effects of steam and electricity were discovered and subjected to man's purposes.

43. Skill is needed to manufacture the tools and implements in daily, even those in household, use, as well as the more complex machinery employed in manufacturing them.

44. The tools, once produced, skill is required in their use. The bow and arrow, and the rifle, are equally useless in the hands of a man who has no skill to use them. The civilized man, armed with a rifle which he did not know how to use, would be no match for the savage, armed with bow and arrow, who had practised shooting at a mark.

45. INDUSTRY, ECONOMY, KNOWLEDGE and SKILL are now seen to be essential to the production of any considerable quantity of the necessaries and comforts of life. Their prevalence is a condition of hu-

man well-being. On the degree in which they prevail will, in a great measure, depend the happiness of every community. The progress and future happiness of every people must depend on the care with which these qualities are sought to be imparted to the young. With what earnestness, then, should not the boys and girls, for whose improvement in these qualities efforts are being made by their parents and teachers, strive to attain knowledge, and to acquire habits of industry, economy and skill!

CHAPTER III.

DIVISION OF LABOR. INCREASED EFFICIENCY RESULTING FROM. CO-OPERATION. HOUSEHOLD LABORS. TRAINING OF THE YOUNG. SPECIAL FITNESS OF WOMEN FOR CERTAIN LABORS.

46. Division of Labor.—In the early stages of society, whatever object is desired by any of its members is produced directly by himself ; that is to say, (violence and fraud excepted,) by the direction of his own labor to the immediate production of the object desired. But the time of the workman is greatly taken up, and his attention distracted by going from one kind of labor to another, and little skill can be acquired in any. It soon came to be perceived that by each laborer applying himself to one class of production exclusively, the total product would be very much increased ; and each laborer can so apply himself without anxiety or hesitation, when, seeing others do likewise, he knows he can readily procure the other things he needs by exchanging for them the direct products of his own labor.

The canoe of the savage, built by the unassisted labor of himself and family, has to be made in intervals between hunting and fishing ; but when society has so far advanced that one portion of its members will find sufficient food for the rest, whereby these others are enabled to devote themselves exclusively to the building of ships, the rude canoe becomes improved into the sailing vessel with masts and sails, and the sailing vessel in her turn yields to that triumph of American skill and ingenuity, the steamship, or ship propelled by steam. What wonderful skill is expended in the construction of an ocean steamer! How marvellously the shipbuilder co-operates with the farmer in the production of grain ; with the tailor, in the production of clothes ; and with the potter and cutler, in the production of their wares !

The separation of the occupations of men, so that each laborer applies himself exclusively to one kind of labor, is termed " DIVISION OF LABOR."

47. Resulting increase in efficiency of labor.—But for it, the acquirement of the knowledge and skill needed for the invention and construction of the steam-engine, of telegraphs, nay, even of comfortable dwellings or clothes, would have been impossible.

The addition made, by the adoption of the division of labor, to the production of man's labor, is doubtless greatest in those industrial occupations which have for their object to supply the more pressing needs of the community ; but its advantages can perhaps be more vividly realized by observing the process of the manufacture of some more trifling kind, such as the illustration given by Adam Smith, in his "Wealth of Nations." "A workman," says Adam Smith, "not educated to the trade" (pinmaking,) "will with difficulty make a dozen pins a day ; " but not only is pinmaking a special business, it is " also divided into branches, each of which is a trade " by itself. One man draws the wire, a second " straightens it, a third cuts, and a fourth points it ; " a fifth grinds the tops to receive the head, while " the making of the head is divided into several

" trades; another workman puts on the head; and
" to whiten the pins, and even to place or stick them
" on papers, is each a separate trade."

The manufactory examined by Adam Smith is
described by him as having been very poor, employing but ten hands, and furnished with indifferent
machinery, and yet they could turn out 12 lbs. of
pins per day. Four thousand medium-sized pins go
to the lb., making 48,000 pins as the day's work of
ten men, whose united product, unaided by division
of labor and co-operation, would not exceed 120 pins
a day !

By the improved machinery of the present day—
results of the still greater division of labor and
more intimate and trustworthy co-operation now in
use—the same number of men can now turn out
over one million of pins a day.

48. In other arts and manufactures the results of
the division of labor are not less striking.

Pin-makers, spinners, weavers, tailors, shoe-mak-
ers, architects, lawyers, builders, and engineers, not
one whit less than the farmers, all *co-operate* to
provide wholesome and palatable food, comfortable
clothing, and abundant fuel and shelter for all.
Each co-operates in the labor of every other industrial worker ; and the lessons of economy shown in

the last chapter receive additional enforcement from the observation of the fact, that all these laborers are living while they labor, on the products of past labor. How enormous, then, must have been the amount of *saving* which has been going on in the past, and which is essential in the present and for the future!

There is one class of labor on which it is desirable to devote some attention, because its importance and position in the economy of industrial life are frequently overlooked.

49. Household labors.—The household labors, generally performed by females, are no whit less honorable, essential, or productive than any labor performed by man. If these labors were not performed for the men, they would have to do them for themselves, and, from want of experience, they would neither be done so well nor so quickly as they are now. The labors, too, now performed by men would be constantly interrupted, and, consequently, be less skilfully performed, and their labor be less productive than at present.

Hence domestic workers, whether men or women, co-operate in the building of bridges, railroads, ships, and, in short in the production of all commodities whatever.

50. The training of the young is a class of labor which nature has specially pointed out as best performed by women, and there is little doubt but that the special fitness of women for training the young, requiring woman's constant presence in the home, has caused the chief portion of domestic labor to continue, even in civilized communities, to fall to her lot.

51. In our country this special fitness of women to train the young has received a further development.

52. The high and noble vocation of the teacher is chiefly filled by women among us. They carry into the school the qualities and faculties which especially adapt that sex for the training of the young; and they are undoubtedly better able to understand the wants and feelings of children than less sympathizing man.

CHAPTER IV.

INTERCHANGE. NECESSITY OF CONSIDERING AND SATISFYING THE
WANTS OF OTHERS.

53. *Interchange.*—The adoption of the division of labor throws a new duty on the laborer. He has no longer to consider what he himself needs in order to supply his wants, but he must ascertain what things are most desired by other producers.

54. Having ascertained this, he knows that other producers will be as anxious to exchange their products for his as he will be to acquire theirs, and he can devote his whole skill and energy to the production of his one commodity.

55. The quantity of the commodities he needs, which he will be able to procure, (skill, industry and economy being supposed equal,) will be proportioned to the judgment he has exercised in supplying the wants of others.

56. *Harmony of Industries.*—The beautiful harmony of industries which here comes in view deserves our especial consideration.

A man's own happiness is his only motive to action, that is to say, the gratification of some one or more of his faculties is what induces man to act. Even when moved to action by sympathy for others, as, for instance, for members of his own family, it is still to gratify his own sympathetic organs or facul-- ties that he acts, as these organs would be pained did he not do so. He balances, (unconsciously in most cases,) the pain of the labor he gives himself to do good to those dear to him, against the pain he would suffer if he failed to do so, and finding the latter would be greater than the former, gratifies himself by performing the act which is to make another happy. This is a fact, nay, a truism, which folly and ignorance may deplore, but which knowl- edge observes to be as much a part of man's nature and as necessary to the preservation of the species as are his appetites.

57. For if man were not guided by the desire for his own happiness, to gratify his own desires, but each man's actions were dictated by what he con- ceived to be the wants of another, instead of men eating when hungry and laboring to avoid starva- tion, endeavoring to avoid being frozen by cold or burnt by fire, they would perish for want of food, or from cold, or fire, while awaiting the provision or salvation to be provided them by another, and the

entire human race would soon disappear from the earth.

58. The desire we have to procure for ourselves ·and those dear to us as large a supply as possible of the necessaries and comforts of life, can be gratified only by supplying the wants of others, thus blending in a common bond the interests of all, and making the welfare of each industrial worker identical with that of the community in which he labors.

————

CHAPTER V.

PROTECTION TO LIFE AND PROPERTY. HONESTY. SMALL EFFI-
CIENCY OF GOVERNMENTS. CONSCIENCE THE MOST EFFICIENT
POLICE. EFFECTS OF DISHONESTY. DEMORALIZING INFLUENCE
OF UCCESSFUL DISHONESTY.

59. Protection.—We have seen that the means of subsistence and of enjoyment can only be procured by labor, and that industry, knowledge, skill and economy are essential to their production and preservation. But man devotes himself to labor to satisfy his needs, and having produced, he must be permitted to enjoy ; otherwise he would soon grow tired of his useless toil, and, production ceasing, the world would be filled with misery. Famine and pestilence would soon sweep from the earth a race which failed to insure to industry the property it had acquired by labor.

60. To secure to the laborer the enjoyment of what he has produced by his labor is, then, one of the earliest efforts of society emerging from barbarism. *Protection to property must be secured,* or the inducement to labor is diminished, and that to save and husband is destroyed. But beyond perceiving the necessity of establishing security for property, man has yet made little progress ; the most civilized societies are yet groping in doubt and uncertainty as to the means best adapted for the attainment of this end.

61. Honesty.—Were all men so organized and so taught and trained in youth, that to seek to obtain possession of the products of another's labor save in exchange for that of their own, should be revolting to their own minds, the difficulty would cease to exist.

62. Unhappily, some there are who, from defective training or organization, seek to obtain the products of labor by other means than working and saving—viz., by violence or fraud ; and from their

efforts it is greatly to be desired that the workers should be protected.

With this object in view, governments have been established, police and courts of justice have been organized, and for the support of those serving in these offices, *Taxes* are levied and collected.

63. But taxes can be gotten only from the earnings of the industrious and saving, and even if the functions of police and magistrates were performed to perfection, the reward and consequent inducement to the industrious and saving, to labor and to save, must be diminished by the amount taken from them in taxes to pay the labors of magistrates and police.

64. Unhappily, we are here met by a still graver difficulty; not only are the functions ascribed to police and magistrates not performed to perfection, but in the most advanced societies yet established, the system of laws and of justice are so imperfect, that it is a grave question whether the benefits secured by magistrates and police are adequate to the cost of maintaining them.

65. Conscience the most effective police. —Whatever means may, as civilization progresses, be finally accepted as best adapted to afford security for property, one thing at least is clear: the

larger the number of those who adopt violence or
fraud as a means to procure wealth, the larger needs
to be the force employed to resist them, the greater
the cost of maintaining such force, and the greater
the risk, always great, of finding the protective force
itself invaded by the presence, in its own bosom, of
the violent or fraudulent. *No police nor magistrate
can be so constant, vigilant, or efficient as that which the
well-trained citizen carries always about with him—viz.,
his own conscience.*

Hence the only means which can, in our present
state of civilization, be relied on as *certain* to add to
the security of property, are *individual character and
self-control,* to be secured only by good teaching and
training in youth.

66. Although the necessity for honesty has been
evolved in our investigation, posteriorly in scientific
order to industry, skill and economy, none of the
last-named qualities can ever flourish in the absence
of respect for property; while, as the natural in-
stinct of man is to *take* what he sees and desires
until he learns the evil consequences of so doing, the
exercise of this quality of honesty needs to be earliest taught. It needs training and experience for
youth to learn the many forms under which honesty
should be exercised, until it grows into a habit of

mind, a part of his nature, a permanent quality of character.

The advantages derivable from a division of labor would be wholly lost to us in the absence of trustworthiness and truthfulness. Some amount of these qualities is absolutely indispensable for the adoption of the division of labor at all; its full benefits can never be realized while falsehood. or any species of fraud or untrustworthiness prevails among us.

67. It is not alone by diminishing the inducement to labor and economy that society is injured by the practices of the dishonest. In all civilized countries, while the industrious and saving are consuming, they are, as we have seen, replacing, not only what they consume, but what is consumed by the sick, the maimed, and the incapable; and, in addition, are increasing the store of wealth of the community year by year.

The dishonest, the rogues, the cheats and thieves who plague society, also consume, and that without replacing what they consume; they also frequently destroy as much as they enjoy.

68. If society submitted without resistance to the depredations of the dishonest, it would fall back into misery and barbarism, so that there would be little left for the thieves to steal; it is therefore best, even

for the subsistence of the thief himself, that his efforts should be resisted, and himself restrained from his evil courses. But while endeavoring to secure the rights of property, we must be careful not to exaggerate the capabilities of the best of governments.

69. Government can strive to provide security for wealth, *but it cannot create it.*

70. Wealth is the product of industry, skill, knowledge and economy. In so far as governments succeed in affording security for life, liberty and property, in so far it promotes these virtues ; but the fundamental qualities of civilized man can be secured only by good teaching and training in youth, the most important part whereof is the home influence of the parents. If, then, the parents possess these virtues, we may hope to see them reproduced in a yet greater degree in their children; and as the seeds of these qualities must be sown in infancy, it is in infancy we must begin the training to make good parents.

71. Demoralizing influence on the witnesses of dishonest examples.—Besides the direct discouragement to industry occasioned by dishonesty, it has yet another influence which, though indirect, is far more pernicious than its direct influence. This indirect influence consists in the demoralization which it occasions in the minds of those who perceive crime enjoying that success which should only be the reward of industry, skill and trustworthiness.

72. Let us carefully guard ourselves against yielding approval or respect in any form to wrong-doing, no matter how successful or powerful it may be, but, on the contrary, let it receive at all times our unqualified scorn, and a hatred proportioned to its success.

CHAPTER VI.

THE YOUNG NOT POSSESSED OF WEALTH. THEIR WANTS SUPPLIED. SALE AND PURCHASE OF LABOR. SELLERS OF LABOR AND NOT THE WEALTH POSSESSORS HAVE THE ENJOYMENT OF THE PORTION OF THE LATTER'S WEALTH EMPLOYED IN PRODUCTION. WAGES. CAPITAL. INTEREST. AVERAGE WAGES DETERMINED BY PRODUCTIVENESS. INDIVIDUAL WAGES; HOW DETERMINED

73. As a rule, the young are not possessed of wealth; yet their wants are regularly supplied. Some parents, it is true, owing in most cases to defective teaching and training in their youth, are not so able or willing as others to supply their children's

needs. By giving the young such education as shall render them self-supporting, and shall hinder them from undertaking the parental duties until they have made provision for the maintenance of a family, the number of incapable or unwilling parents will be diminished in the future. Children whose misfortune it is to be neglected by their parents, generally suffer through life the consequences of such neglect, though their sufferings are often mitigated in childhood by the charity of society or of individuals.

74. But though the wealth-possessors may be willing to part with a portion of their wealth for the relief of destitute children, as also of incapable or disabled adults, they are not willing to give of their wealth to adults who are neither incapable nor disabled, except in return for some services rendered or to be rendered by the latter.

75. *Sale and purchase of labor.*—Happily a means exists by which they who have no wealth saved up for their immediate wants can induce the wealth possessors to part cheerfully with theirs. The former can sell their labor to the latter: *i. e.*, give the wealth possessors the right to the future product of their present labor, in exchange for the present wealth of which they stand in need. This can be done because most of the wealth-possessors are anxious to increase their wealth.

76. How the wealthless have the enjoyment of the wealth of its possessors.—The wealth-possessors might choose to retain their wealth for their own consumption. In parting with it to laborers, they allow the latter to consume it in their stead. The laborers, then, and not the wealth-possessors, have the enjoyment of the wealth the latter employ in the purchase of labor, and the wealth-possessors cheerfully part with their wealth in the hope that the products of the labor they purchase will replace the wealth they have bestowed upon the laborer, *with an increase thereto.*

77. Wages and Capital.—The price of the labor purchased by the wealth possessor is termed WAGES; the portion of wealth employed or destined to be employed in the production of fresh wealth is termed CAPITAL, and the owners thereof CAPITALISTS. The wealth employed in the payment of wages, is obviously a part of capital.

78. Many persons are both capitalists and laborers. He who possesses skill as a workman, and who in the course of years of industry, and of saving, has made a provision for himself and family, may yet lack the talent successfully to administer his capital, and conscious of his incapacity, may prefer to lend it to other more capable administrators, (as by

depositing it in a savings bank,) in return for a fixed payment, to be made at stated intervals, by the latter.

This sum, such administrators agree to pay, *hoping* to do so out of the profits they may earn from administering such borrowed capital.

79. *Interest*.—This fixed payment is called IN-TEREST.

The laws of nature by which its amount is fixed, will be hereafter investigated.

80. Again the capitalist-laborer may become a stockholder in some joint stock company, sharing in the risk, but not in the labor of administration, while continuing to sell his own labor for wages as theretofore.

81. As already intimated, the wages paid by the capitalist do not comprise the whole of that portion of wealth which is employed or destined to be employed productively. The various tools and aids to industry, plant and machinery, ships, docks, railroads, flax, cotton, wool, hides, etc., produced by labor, and destined to be employed in further production, are also capital, and it is because it is desired to consider phenomena common to all those portions of wealth which are destined for employment in the production of wealth, that the things embraced

in that idea, are classed together in a common name, viz: CAPITAL.

82. Average Wages.—Wages are paid out of existing capital; but it is the average productiveness of labor, which ultimately determines the average rate of wages. If we suppose the supply of capital in any particular trade to have become small, compared with the number of highly skilled laborers. the wages paid to each laborer must be small also. But the unusual profit attending capital employed in that trade would speedily attract to it capital from other trades and countries, and a higher rate of wages would be paid, until the efficiency of the laborer would be fully remunerated. Hence it is *the productiveness of labor,* in any given community, which ultimately determines the average rate of wages.

83. In Mr. Brassey's work, entitled . "Work and Wages Practically Illustrated," evidence will be found, showing this law to hold good, not only between rates of wages in any one community, but even as between different communities.

Notwithstanding the great and striking diversities in the rates of wages in different communities, the cost of a given amount of the products of labor is everywhere about the same! As a result, Mr. Brassey found that in Italy, Moldavia, or in India, any piece of engineering work could be constructed as cheaply by English as by native laborers—that is to say, that notwithstanding the higher rates of wages paid to British laborers, the greater efficiency of their labor rendered it equally profitable to employ them as to employ the natives.

This result, so totally at variance with popular notions upon the subject, is precisely what was predicated by the scientific observer; and since the inferior laborers have to provide subsistence for themselves and those dependent upon them out of their wages no less than the more efficient laborer, it is obvious how greatly an increase in the efficiency of the laborers must promote *their* well-being.

84. Individual wages.—We have now to consider what causes determine the rate of individual wages, and the operation of those causes.

The laborer desires to sell his labor to the best advantage; the purchaser desires to secure the greatest amount of future products in return for his present outlay. Hence he will seek for the industrious and skilful laborer in preference to the slothful or ignorant, the honest to the dishonest, the careful, trustworthy and sober to the careless, unpunctual

and drunken. The unhappy beings who are subject
to the infirmities of dishonesty, idleness, ignorance,
carelessness or drunkenness, either will get no employment, or, at best, must sell their labor at a lower
rate than their better disposed and better trained
comrades, because the capitalist can only afford to
purchase their labor at a rate of wages such as shall
enable him to employ more than ordinarily efficient
foremen to prevent or correct the mischiefs which
the misconduct of the ill-trained laborers might
otherwise occasion.

He must also himself be compensated for the additional anxiety and labor the employment of such
workmen occasion him, as well as the risk incurred,
amounting to an actual percentage of loss, which the
diligence of himself and superintendent will fail to
avert.

85. The application of these principles to daily
life is not difficult. Clearly, they who do most work
must, when paid by the piece, receive most wages;
when paid by the day, those who work the greater
number of days will receive more in a year than they
who work fewer. The former, becoming known as
reliable and punctual workmen, and year by year
acquiring greater skill in consequence of unintermit-
ted labor, gain a character which causes them to be

sought after by capitalists, and so insure to themselves more constant employment or a higher rate of wages, and generally both combined.

Neither does the additional share the better conducted laborers receive leave a smaller amount for distribution among the less well-conducted.

While establishing the character which enables the well-conducted laborer to command a rate of wages above the average, he was temporarily receiving *less*, in proportion to the productiveness of his labor, than his fellow-workman. He consequently yielded a larger return to the capitalist than they, and thus added to the fund from which wages are paid, which, at the time he receives his enhanced wages, is greater than it would have been by reason of his former conduct; and he now only draws a portion of that addition which the superior productiveness of his past labor has added to it, the residue being distributed by capitalists among other laborers.

86. Neither is this the only advantage to the less fortunate laborers. Placed under the watchful eyes of trustworthy overlookers, opportunity is given them to acquire that skill and industry in which they are deficient, while the difference between their wages and that of the better conducted workmen,

affords them an inducement to grow out of bad habits into good ones.

87. How wages may be increased.—Improvement, then, in the conduct of laborers is the most powerful means by which the productiveness of labor, and consequently its remuneration, can be increased.

88. Wages proportioned to conduct.—We thus perceive, that other things being equal, the wages earned by individual laborers is *proportioned to their conduct,* furnishing another instance of that harmony of nature whose action, when uninterrupted by man's ignorance, tends to encourage and develop those qualities which most conduce to human well-being.

89. Circumstances affecting wages in different trades.—There are yet other considerations which affect the rates of wages of different occupations. Some trades are easy, others severe, some healthy, others unhealthy, some safe, others dangerous, some constant, others intermittent, some attractive, and others repulsive. The preference which all laborers will give to the easy, healthy, safe, constant and attractive labor, can only be overcome by the offer of higher wages in the severe, unhealthy, dangerous, intermittent or repulsive.

90. In this favored country there are few trades in which diligence and economy will not secure a

comfortable living to the workman, and at the least
a tolerable competence for old age ; hence the choice
of employment to which one about to commence his
industrial career should be directed, may generally
be safely left to be determined by his tastes and in-
clinations.

" But the selection of an employer is of great importance, and not more so on account of the influence of the employer himself than of the workmen
he employs ; for as these will be probably for years
the companion of the new-comer, the selection of an
employer who endeavors to employ the best workmen should be the first thought of the parent or
guardian whose child or ward is about entering on
his industrial career.

91. "Should circumstances arise whereby a good
workman happens to be thrown into the employment of a bad employer, the latter is not bound to
stay beyond the term of service contracted for, and
his leaving will be wise, provided he has a reasonable prospect of bettering his condition. This he may
be enabled to do either by being invited by other
employers, or by seeking them, or he may resolve to
employ himself.

"To be invited by other employers, he must have
established a reputation for usefulness ; to be suc-

cessful in seeking better employment, he must be able to offer evidence of work previously performed, while to employ himself he must have acquired the qualifications necessary for the successful administration of capital, and must have saved from his past earnings the capital necessary for the subsistence of himself and the workmen he employs until the produce of that labor can be realized in the market."*

92. It is thus clear that the workmen who suffer from insufficiency of wages should look to their own deficiency in one or more of the industrial virtues as the cause, and to correct such defects as the efficient means for attaining good wages.

93. Especially is this true in countries so happily situated as our own. However unsatisfactory may be the present condition of any working man, a short period of probation and labor under the guidance of a skilled farmer will suffice for him to acquire the knowledge and skill necessary for successfully farming a few acres of the unoccupied fertile land of this continent, and he can then betake himself to a calling where the return for his labor and capital will, if combined with thrift, soon place him in a position of secure and permanent well-being.

---

* Quoted from memory from Ellis's "Phenomena of Social Life."

CHAPTER VII.

Profit. Its uncertainty. Analysis of. Rates, how determined. Capital the best friend of labor.

94. Profit.—The owner of wealth is induced to
employ his wealth as capital in the hope of thereby
procuring an increase to his stock.

The laborer, when he takes some of the savings
of his past labor, and exchanges it, say for a spade,
is a capitalist to that extent, and makes the conversion in the expectation that he will thereby be able
to earn more in the future; that the spade will add
to the productiveness of his future labor. The farmer who purchases a plough, a barrow, a reaping or
threshing machine, expects that the wealth thus applied to the purpose of production will, before the
implement be worn out, be returned to him with an
increase. The purchaser of labor expects that the
products of the labor, the right to which he has purchased, will replace to him the wealth paid for it,
with an increase. The increase thus expected by
the capitalist, whether upon his outlay for a spade,
buildings, machinery, or wages, is, *when realized*,
termed PROFIT; it is the hope of profit which induces

the owner of wealth to employ it in production. But this hope may not be realized. The wages of the laborer are in hand and certain, but the profit of the employer is in the future and uncertain. He pays wages out of wealth he actually possesses. The wealth by which the wages thus advanced is to be replaced, as well as to yield the hoped-for profit, has yet to be produced. Crops sometimes fail, cattle may perish, fires destroy, or mistakes may sweep away the whole or a great part of the anticipated product of the labor for which present wealth has been expended. The average of profit must therefore be sufficient to counterbalance these risks, or wealth will cease to be converted into capital. It must also give to the capitalist, as administrator, a remuneration equal to what he could earn by selling his labor.

95. Analysis of profit.—Profit, then, may be resolved into three elements :

(1.) *Remuneration* for the *skill and labor* of the capitalist as administrator.

(2.) *Remuneration* for the *risk of loss* he incurs as owner of the capital, or insurance.

(3.) *Remuneration* for his having *abstained from consuming ;* in other words, remuneration for the use of his capital, to which last the name of INTEREST has been applied.

96. If now any particular calling offered, to those engaged in it, a larger profit, in proportion to the skill and labor necessary for its prosecution, to its attractiveness, and to the risks attending it, than other callings, other capitalists would seek to embark their capital in it, or those engaged in it would continually increase their capital, until the rate of profit were reduced to something approaching uniformity.

97. Qualifications of a Capitalist.—The most important qualification for a successful capitalist, will be a combination of economy with an administrative capacity, such as shall enable him to direct the labor he purchases, so as to yield the largest profit; to select the most efficient laborers, and attract them to his service, by offering them the largest wages.

98. Of the profit he makes through his judicious direction of the labor he has purchased, his economy teaches him to save the utmost, so that he may be able to earn a further profit, by adding it to his former capital, and employing the total as capital, by fresh purchases of labor. Punctual and trustworthy in fulfilling his own engagements, he possesses judgment to entrust only to punctual and trustworthy customers, and agents, the wealth he administers. He who possesses less discrimination

3*

of character, either in the selection of laborers and
the wages he pays, or in the direction he gives to
their labor, or in the choice of his customers and
agents, or is himself wanting in economy, or trustworthiness, receives a smaller return upon the labor
he directed, or is less saving of it when obtained.
He therefore fails to increase the fund, out of which
wages are paid, to the extent done by the capitalist
who makes larger profit, and we thus perceive that
*the larger the profits made by the capitalist the greater
is the benefit, not only to himself, but, chief of all, to the
laborer.* Hence again, the laborer should strive to
make his labor as productive as possible to his employer, as the surest means of increasing his own
wages.

99. When to this consideration is added, the
strengthening of those good habits in the laborer,
on which we have seen his wages so much depend,
as well as the earning a character for their possession, the importance to the laborer of rendering his
labor as productive as he can, cannot be over-esti-
mated. Hence the interests of the capitalist, and
of the laborer, are coincident.

100. We sometimes hear capital spoken of as the
enemy of labor. We now see it is its best friend.
Capital in the hands of the capitalist, is far more

useful to the laborer, than to the owner. The latter enjoys the possible and probable, but by no means certain profit in the future, the *laborers have the present use of the entire capital employed in the purchase of labor*, while, to the owner, his capital is of use only as a provision against future need, to the laborer it furnishes the means of present subsistance, without which, he, and those dear to him must perish for want.

CHAPTER VIII.

PROPERTY IN LAND. RENT. HOW REGULATED.

101. Property in land.—In a previous chapter the right of property in the products of labor was found to be a law of nature, discovered by observing man's wants and character, and the necessity, thence resulting, of giving encouragement to labor; we notice also everywhere a right of property in land and we have now to consider whether such a right is justifiable.

102. The case is well stated in Mr. Opdyke's little work on political economy :

He supposes the members of a community " pos-" sessed of a right common to each to partake of the " utility derivable from the soil. They mutually " agree to surrender to the mass that common right, " and to accept in its stead the exclusive right to de-" finitive portions."

103. Evidently there is no injustice here, and whether we consider a savage or a civilized society, the immense advantage which accrues to all from the adoption of this rule will become apparent.

104. In the savage state, man, as a hunter, re-quires at the least seven square miles of territory for the support of each member of the tribe. Let us suppose one of them to offer to surrender his right over the ground now held in common by the tribe, on condition of receiving an exclusive right to, not seven square miles, but one or two hundred acres of land only.

This exclusive right being granted to him, al-though the total area of hunting ground is diminished by a few hundred acres, the average for each mem-ber of the tribe is increased, while the settler de-votes himself to the production of commodities which will not only provide a greater amount of comfort for himself and family, but will also yield a surplus store, which may some day serve to support other members of the tribe should a failure of the hunting season threaten them with starvation.

105. The case is not less strong with civilized societies. The pioneer who clears the forest would find no inducement to do so if another could obtain the land he had cleared. The farmer would have little encouragement to turn up the soil and sow the seed, and still less to enclose, manure, or irrigate his field, if, even after he had gathered in his harvest, another could appropriate the improvements he had made.

106. We have seen that all production is but changing the position of matter so as to vary its form or change its place. The pioneer, farmer, miner and builder do the same. They, too, change the position of matter, and in so doing clear the forest, enclose, drain, irrigate, manure and cultivate the field, open shafts and mines, build houses and factories; and they cannot receive back all the products of their labor because part of it remains fixed in the soil in the shape of improved fertility, or other convenience or aid to industry. By their labors they have rendered future labor more productive, and to them, therefore, should be reserved the use

of the implement whose virtues they have discovered
and enhanced, or all would be discouraged from like
effort in the future, and progress would be arrested.

The right, then, to property in land improved
by man's labor, is now seen to have the same
foundation as the right to any other species of property, subject however, to a special liability to taxation for objects common to the whole community, to
be presently explained.

107. Rent.—Let us suppose that into a community where land has been utilized and improved,
there should enter a stranger desirous of applying
his industry to land.   It will be of little consequence
to him whether he take up new land, or pay to the
owner for the use of land already improved the difference between the larger production of the latter
and the smaller production of the former.

The feeling of and desire for ownership might
tempt him to the former; the greater comfort and
certainty would incline him to the latter, and the
scale would probably be turned by the owner of the
improved land offering to let it to him for something
less than the entire additional produce.

The amount he pays to the landowner for the use
of his improved land is termed " RENT."

108. The amount of the rent the cultivator will be

willing to pay for the use of land will vary greatly with circumstances. In our own country, where millions of acres of fertile land can be had for next to nothing, convenience of situation, proximity to a market, and general accessibility will bo the first consideration.·

109. Let us suppose two classes of lands to be in cultivation, one situated in New Jersey yields, suppose, to the cultivator, 200 barrels of flour, with a given expenditure of labor and capital, and costs 30 barrels for transportation to market, and exchanging for such objects of utility as the farmer desires. Suppose another, situated in the interior of the State of Illinois, yields to the cultivator 300 barrels, upon the like expenditure of labor and capital, but costs him 200 barrels for transportation, and expenses of exchanging his products, it is obvious that tho Illinois farmer could afford to pay 50 barrels for the use of the New Jersey farm, and be 20 barrels the better off for the operation.

110. Let us now suppose the increasing population and requirements of society to render necessary the cultivation of other land, which, whether more or less fertile, than any other of those already in cultivation, will yield to the cultivator for the same expenditure of labor and capital, a *net* return of only

80 barrels. He could evidently afford to pay something less than 20 barrels as rent for the use of the Illinois farm, or something less than 90 barrels as rent for the use of that in New Jersey, rather than take up the third description of land.

But as the increasing population requires the crop of the latter, they must pay a price for it, sufficient to make the cultivation of it profitable, and this price per bushel being higher than the rate hitherto paid for the produce of the more fertile land, the owners of the first and second descriptions of land, will be able to collect a rent nearly equal to the difference in the respective superiorities of those lands over the third land.

111. Precisely the same process goes on with stores and houses in cities, the rents whereof increase with the eligibility of their situation for earning profit or for enjoyment.

For the least eligibly situated stores a rent is obtainable rarely sufficient to pay the interest upon the capital expended in their erection, but as the growth of the city adds to the once least eligible situations, a capacity for earning profit, these in turn cease to be the "least eligible," and command a higher rent for the same capital.

112. Rent, it must now be apparent, *cannot be the*

cause of dearness, or difficulty of production. It may be a consequence, but cannot be a cause of such comparative difficulty or facility. It is a result or consequence of the necessity to which the increasing wants of society have given rise, of having recourse to lands, the net return from which is less for the same expenditure of labor and capital, than lands previously occupied. When the increased fertility or accessibility of land, is the result of labor and skill, then RENT is merely a profit on capital, but when it arises from the growth of population, rendering it neccessary to resort to less fertile or convenient lands, RENT becomes a share in the general product of industry, and if it could be separated from the return earned by skill and labor, would properly belong to the community. RENT is therefore a fitting subject for taxation, within such limits as shall take only such portion as has not accrued through such skill and labor, as above mentioned.

113. If now, among the applicants for a farm or store, one man of superior skill or sagacity, perceives how to obtain a larger return than others, he will offer a higher rent to secure it.

Thus the farm or store comes into the occupancy of him who can by judicious administration, obtain the largest return for the same expenditure of capital and labor, benefitting alike himself and the community. This furnishes yet another illustration of those beautiful harmonies of nature, of which so many instances have already appeared in the course of our investigations into the conditions of human well being.

114. In the more densely peopled countries of the old world, rent, though dependent on the same principles, runs a somewhat different course. Except in the case of offices, stores, warehouses, wharves and other places of business, and of residences in cities, eligibility of situation will be subordinate to the question of fertility of the soil or productiveness of the mine. The means of inter-communication are generally sufficiently good to render the cost of transport and of agency in exchanging so small, that it is of comparatively little consequence whether a farm or mine be situated at fifty or two hundred miles from the market. The abundance of roads renders the entire area around the market of nearly equal eligibility, instead of the practicable farms being, as with us, confined to the margins of a few roads, though even in the most civilized parts of Europe, land bordering on a railroad or navigable river will command a sensibly higher rent than land of the same degree of fertility a few miles distant.

115. The greater area of productive cultivation in Europe, consequent on the whole circle around the market being nearly equally eligible, while we are continually confined to a narrow strip bordering a road, serves to illustrate the truth that it is not desirable to offer any inducements to capitalists to construct roads in advance of the natural wants of the community.

116. The tendency of lands to fall into the hands of those capable of employing them most productively, which we have seen to be the case when people are left free to seek what they deem most to their advantage, leads also to another conclusion; viz., that it cannot be the " extortion or avarice of landlords " which causes a rise in rents; the real cause is the increased wants of the community ; the immediate or proximate cause, the desire of the most capable tenants to secure the means of turning their capacity to the best advantage. The desire of the landlords on the contrary to secure the best tenants, tends to lower rents. Hence the mis-called " grasping of landlords " so far as it has any effect at all, is in the reverse direction to that which is popularly ascribed to it, viz., it tends to lower instead of raising rents.

CHAPTER IX.

VALUE. DEMAND AND SUPPLY. INTRINSIC VALUE A VERBAL CON-
TRADICTION. VALUE, HOW DETERMINED. MARKET VALUE.
SPECULATORS. AVERAGE VALUE. COST OF REPRODUCTION.
LABOR AND UTILITY ESSENTIAL TO VALUE.

117, Value.—The laborer's share in the products
of labor is, we have seen, generally received by him in
advance, and should be apportioned among laborers
in proportion to their capacity for production. If
the capitalist fail so to apportion his capital, the loss
falls upon him. Further, the commodity he produces is intended to be exchanged for others and if he
fail to produce what others desire, he will be unable
to obtain from them what he requires.

The quantity of other commodities or services
which he can obtain in exchange for what he produces, or is about to produce, must be constantly in
the mind of every laborer or director of capital, and
this quantity is the VALUE of the commodity or service about to be exchanged *measured* in those other
commodities or services.

118. Hence value is the quality of being able to
be exchanged for some object of utility or for ser-

vices, and it is measured by the quantity of other
commodities or services obtainable in exchange for
the commodities or services to be disposed of.

**119. *Intrinsic value.*—In ordinary language
the word VALUE is employed to denote, not the quality of exchangeability, but the quantity which measures that quality, and used in this sense there can
be no such thing as "INTRINSIC VALUE."

Used in this sense, there can be no value except
in relation to other things, while the word "intrinsic" implies a quality existing in the object itself.

120. Gold is valuable, malleable, yellow and heavy.
Its yellowness is an attribute which, (light being assumed present,) may be regarded as *intrinsic.* So
with its malleability and weight, for though to measure these qualities, the gold is referred to some
standard, the actual malleability and weight are
qualities *intrinsic* to the gold. Its value, however,
has no existence except in relation to other commodities, and the quality and amount of that value
change not only with every commodity with which
the gold is being compared, but with any one commodity in different circumstances of time, place or
possession.

**121. *Value, how determined.*—Suppose two
persons, A and B, one of whom, suppose A, is

able to produce fifteen hats in a given time
with a given expenditure of labor and capital,
and that with the same expenditure he could produce five pairs of pants, while the other, B, could
produce fifteen pairs of pants with the like expenditure, but only five hats—*i. e.*, A's production equals
fifteen hats or five pairs of pants; B's production
equals five hats or fifteen pairs of pants—it is obvious that A could exchange ten of his hats against
ten of B's pants, and each be five hats and five pairs
of pants better off for the exchange.

122. Suppose two boys, one of whom possesses a
penknife and the other a bag of marbles; the boy
who owns the penknife wishes to play at marbles,
and the owner of the marbles wants to cut a boat
out of a block of wood ; they can exchange the penknife against the marbles ; each gratifies his desire,
and the value of the penknife measured in marbles,
as estimated by both of them, is the bag in question,
and the value of the bag of marbles is the penknife.
In this case, each boy measures the gratification he
anticipates to derive from the thing he is to receive,
calculates whether he could get the same enjoyment
by a less sacrifice than that of all the enjoyment he
might derive from the thing he gives in exchange,
and arriving at the conclusion that he will derive

greater enjoyment from the thing he is to receive than from that with which he is about to part, and that he could not get the same enjoyment at a less cost, he consummates the exchange, and each is the gainer by the excess of gratification he derives from the thing he now possesses over what he believed that he might have derived from the thing with which he has parted.

123. Suppose, now, a surgeon to be called in by a miller to set a broken arm. He performs a service. He needs flour for his family, and accepts in exchange say twenty sacks of flour. To obtain the flour the miller built his mill and ground wheat or other grain for the farmer. *The reward for the services thus rendered by him he now makes over to the surgeon in exchange for the service of setting the broken limb.*

Or the surgeon may visit the family of a lawyer, give his *services* in endeavoring to heal the lawyer or some member of his family, and may receive, in exchange for his services, some legal information or assistance—*i. e., service*—from the lawyer.

124. Two persons about effecting an exchange estimate the amount of labor and capital each would have to devote to obtain the commodity, or yield the service required, and establish between them the value of each commodity or service measured in the other as the result of such estimate.

125. The one commodity or service may have cost more time, labor and capital to any indefinite extent than the other commodity or service, or may possess an enormously greater utility ; if, nevertheless, the owner of the former desires the latter, and could procure it only by a larger expenditure of time, labor and capital than it would cost him to reproduce his own commodity, he will gladly consent to exchange the former for the latter, and so establish its value as measured in his commodity.

126. Value then results from the estimate formed by two or more persons about to effect an exchange of the satisfaction from the service or commodity to be disposed of by each other, and is measured by the quantity of other commodities or services given in exchange for the commodity or service to be disposed of.

127. Market Value.—As in consequence of the adoption of the division of labor, each producer must, to get what he desires, produce what is desired by other people, the question arises how is the intending producer to know what commodity is likely to be most generally desired, and how is the amount of commodities he is to receive, i. e., how is the value of this commodity to be determined? To answer this question in each particular case, requires judgment and experience of the various circumstances and phenomena of the industrial society to which he belongs. A knowledge of the causes of fluctuations of value is indispensable to the acquirement of even a moderate degree of that judgment and experience.

128. Let us suppose a state of the market such that a pair of boots, a pair of pants, two hats, and 100 lbs. of flour would exchange for one another; in other words, that the value of a pair of boots measured in flour shall be 100 lbs., measured in hats shall be two hats, and measured in pants shall be one pair, and conversely that the value of 100 lbs. of flour measured in boots or pants shall be one pair, or measured in hats shall be two hats.

Suppose now, while everything else remained the same, the quantity of one commodity, say boots, were to be increased; then they who had boots to give in exchange would obtain, for each pair of boots, less in exchange than they had obtained before; boots would fall in value owing to the increased supply, and all other commodities would rise in value measured in boots.

129. Let us now suppose, other things remaining the same, the desire for boots to be diminished, the boot owners would in such case be compelled to ac-

4

cept less in exchange for each pair of boots; boots would fall in value.

130. In the converse case of an increased desire for boots, the boot owners would receive more in exchange, on account of the desire felt by each person not to be among those who went without. Boots would rise in value, and all other commodities would fall in value measured in boots.   •

131. Among the various commodities which form the objects of man's desires, and are the results of his labor, the *supply* of some is more subject to *vicissitudes* than is that of others. Vegetable productions, which depend so much upon the weather are, as a class, more subject to fluctuations of supply than clothing.

Among the former, fruits popularly so called, and potatoes, being particularly perishable, are subject to greater fluctuations than corn and grain, some surplus of which generally remains from former harvests, while none of the old crops of fruits or potatoes can be preserved, except by subjecting them to a laborious process specially devised for the purpose.

Machinery, factories, ships, roads and houses are less subject to fluctuations of supply than either food or clothing, the former being comparatively durable, so that the annual product forms but a small portion of the entire stock on hand.

This is true in a still more eminent degree of gold and silver, the annual production whereof is very small in comparison with the accumulations on hand.

132. The supply and demand of commodities are greatly affected by anticipations of future supply and demand. Fortunately for mankind a bad harvest is generally preceded by unfavorable weather which causes farmers to keep back supplies. Speculators and merchants scour the country to gather up this store, which but for their exertions, might be brought to market and temporarily keep down the value it is true, but at the risk of converting a short supply into a famine by preventing that rise in price, by which the community would be warned to diminish their consumption, and notice given to the peoples of distant lands that their surplus food would find a profitable market in supplying the deficiency.

If on the other hand the prospects of the coming harvest are favorable, those who have last year's grain on hand will hasten to bring it to market, speculators and merchants postpone their demand to await the forthcoming supply, and when prices have reached their lowest point, they buy it up and preserve for the hour of need what might otherwise be wasted.

133. Speculators.—Contrary to the prejudices still rife amongst the people, we now perceive that honest and honorable *speculators*, are, *when success-ful*, of the greatest service to society, the services they render being, in fact, measured by the profits they realize.

134. We have ascertained that the fluctuations of value depend on the fluctuations of supply and demand, or more correctly expressed, that value is determined by the equation of supply and demand; the term "equation of supply and demand" being used to express the fact of the demand becoming equal to the supply by rising or falling, until the quantity in the market is exactly carried off at the increased or lessened value.

It remains now to investigate the laws which regulate the fluctuations in the supply and demand respectively.

135. Average value.—Each producer seeks to produce the commodity which will enable him to obtain the largest amount of other commodities in return. If on taking a large number of the values obtained for one commodity, say hops, he finds that the average value of the hops he produces is less than that of some other commodity, say wheat, costing the same amount of capital and labor for its production, part of the capital heretofore employed in the production of hops will be employed in producing wheat, or in some other industrial occupation, until the diminished supply of the hops, leading to a rise in their value, shall cause the capital and labor employed in growing them to yield at least an equal return with capital employed in other departments of industry.

Hence, the fluctuations in the equation of supply and demand are subject to the anticipations formed by the administrators of capital of probable future values as compared with the *cost of reproduction.* These anticipations are formed on a computation of average values in the past, and of the circumstances which may affect supply and demand in the future. It is by comparing the *probable average value* thus anticipated with the *cost of reproduction* of a like utility, *i. e.,* of an object capable of supplying the like amount of satisfaction, that the operations for future supply and demand are regulated.

136. *Hence the cost of reproduction of a like utility regulates the average equation of supply to demand, and this cost, therefore, is the regulator of average values.*

137. It is a self-evident conclusion from the fore-

going that *cost,* (*i. e., labor,*) and *utility,* must both concur in the production of a commodity in order that it may possess value.

CHAPTER X.

MEANS OF FACILITATING INTERCHANGE. WEIGHTS AND MEASURES.
MEASURE OF VALUE. MONEY. GOLD AND SILVER. PROPER-
TIES WHICH ADAPT THEM FOR USE AS MONEY. THE DOLLAR.
ABSURDITY OF ATTEMPTS TO FIX BY LAW THE RELATIVE VALUES
OF GOLD AND SILVER. CAUSES OF FLUCTUATIONS IN THE VALUE
OF MONEY.

138. Means of facilitating interchange.
As the division of labor was carried out more and more minutely, interchange assumed greater impor-tance, and means were hit upon for facilitating it.

139. The most important of these means, was the adoption of various standards by which to measure length, surface, cubic contents or capacity, weight, time, heat, and VALUE.

140. The adoption of these standards of measure enables the mind to be set free from any necessity for dwelling upon quantity. Quality and value could now be exclusively considered. The determination of

quality was also in many cases greatly facilitated by the use of one or more of these different measures; while many industries could not have been discovered or invented at all, and we should have continued without the means of enjoyment obtained through them, but for the prior invention and use of these standards of measure.

141. STANDARDS OF MEASURE thus serve both as *labor-saving expedients* and as *instruments whereby labor is rendered more productive.*

Through the assistance they render, the judgment can be concentrated on a few considerations and is thereby rendered more skillful in arriving at just and accurate conclusions.

But to enable the full advantages derivable even from our present systems of measures to be secured, a general prevalence of honesty in their employment is necessary.

142. Unfortunately, there are persons who seek to abuse the confidence reposed in the general accuracy of the various measures in use.

Whatever organization may exist for the detection and punishment of such dishonesty, the strongest safeguard against its occurrence must be the training of the young in habits of thought and in conduct which will lead them to appreciate at its full iniquity the wickedness of such acts, and to estimate at its just weight the burthen thrown upon industry through the increased watchfulness they necessitate, and the check thereby put upon the productiveness of labor.

143. Referring the student to the appropriate works upon the various other measures, we will now proceed to examine one of the chief instruments employed to facilitate interchange—viz., the MEASURE OF VALUE.

The necessity for a common measure of value early presented itself.

It would rarely happen that two persons possessed each what the other needed, in the exact quantities desired, so long as barter remained the only manner in which interchange could be effected. So soon as some object was discovered which all persons would be desirous of having, they would be willing to accept it in exchange for their commodities, because with it they could always obtain, in exchange, the commodities they might need. The object which was found to fulfil this requirement received the name of MONEY.*

144. It is an interesting study to observe the va-

* From "moneta," Latin for adviser.

rious objects which, from time to time, in different ages of man's history, and among different peoples, have been selected to perform the office of a measure of value. One thing in particular must be noted. *As the measure of length must possess length, so must the measure of value possess value.*

145. Now we have seen that cost—*i. e.*, labor and utility, must both concur in the production of a commodity in order that it may possess value; hence whatever be the measure of value adopted, it must be an *object of utility, and must cost labor to produce.*

146. In constructing, and selecting the materials for, the standard measures of length, weight or capacity, so much care as possible has been taken to make them exact and of such material as should be least liable to fluctuations, as from the weather or other causes. So in selecting measures of value, the great desideratum is to find some commodity which should be least subject to be affected by those causes which occasion *fluctuations* in value.

147. After many different materials had been tried, gold or silver was at last hit upon by every civilized nation, mainly from the fact of the *very large stock on hand in comparison with the annual production.*

148. The prominent cause of fluctuations in value,

4*

it will be remembered, is, that of most commodities
the annual product bears a large proportion to the
stock or quantity on hand. While in the case of
gold and silver, (called the precious metals,) their in-
destructibility has caused a very large accummula-
tion compared with the quantity annually produced.
When to this is added the great cost of the production of the precious metals, and the universal demand for them, (in consequence whereof their bulk
is small compared with their value, whereby they are
easily portable,) and that by reason of their ductility
and homogeneousness they can be readily divided and
reduced into pieces of any required shape, weight
and standard of fineness, gold and silver, and gold
in preference to silver, are seen to possess in a su-
perlative degree all the qualities desirable in a measure of value. It must, nevertheless, be remembered
that gold and silver are themselves commodities,
subject to the same laws of value as all other commodities, and that when it is said that a commodity, say corn, has risen in value as measured in gold
or silver, it is the same thing as saying that gold or
silver has fallen in value as measured in corn. The
cause of the fluctuation would, however, have to be
sought rather in a diminished supply of corn than in
any increased supply of gold or silver.

149. But neither gold nor silver is fit to be employed in a pure or unalloyed state.

For the purpose of being used as coin, gold needs to be hardened, and this is best done by the admixture of copper, with a very small percentage of silver.

150. To recapitulate : The qualities which recommend gold or silver as the materials of which the standard of value should be composed are :

(1.) The great estimation in which they are held.

(2.) Portability, *i. e.*, their large value, (consequent on the great cost of their production,) in a comparatively small bulk and weight, as compared with the value of other commodities of given bulk and weight.

(3.) Durability, being almost indestructible.

(4.) Their capacity for receiving an alloy, *i. e.*, for having mixed with them some other metal in any given proportion in such a manner that the whole mass is of a uniform standard of fineness in all its parts, whereby the softness of gold and the brittleness of silver can be modified to any desired degree.

(5.) The smallness of the annual production, compared with the total stock on hand, a property resulting from their durability and great cost of production, and rendering them little susceptible to fluctuations of value when measured in all other commodities.

(6.) Their homogeneousness of structure, or quality

of being alike throughout, whereby they can be readily verified.

(7.) Fusibility.

(8.) Their capacity for readily receiving a delicate impression and faithfully preserving it, which may be termed Coinability.

(9.) Their peculiar sonorousness, *i. e.*, the peculiar ringing sound given out by them when struck, to which sound the name of 'metallic ring' has been given and which affords an easy and generally reliable test of the genuineness of the metal or coin.

151. The *value* of gold and silver, like that of all other commodities depends on supply and demand, but as the principal demands for these metals is to serve as money, substitutes for money have to be taken into consideration in estimating the supply. Now of these substitutes, CREDIT is the chief, and the quantity of gold and silver actually employed, bears in general, (in civilized communities,) hardly so great a proportion to the amount of credit, as the value of the small change in circulation, does to that of gold and silver.

152. The causes which affect the supply and demand of gold and silver, irrespective of alterations in the supply and demand of other commodities *as compared with one another*, are

(1.) An increased supply of commodities arising from the accumulation of savings which will cause an increased demand for money to facilitate exchanges.

(2.) A diminished supply of other commodities arising from waste or destruction which will diminish the demand for money.

(3.) As civilization progresses the demand may be diminished by the disuse of ornaments on the person, from an economical use of gold and silver, and from the general use of substitutes for money.

(4.) An increased demand may arise from an increase in gold or silver objects of utility, or an increased taste for ornament, or from their replacing a debased or inferior currency, or from a widespread feeling of mistrust putting a stop to credit as a substitute for money. In the cases numbered one and four the value of money will rise, in those numbered two and three the value of money will fall.

153. Money being, as we now perceive, merely a a means of facilitating the interchange of commodities, the mere measure of value, as other measures measure time, length, surface, capacity, weight, or heat; an increase in the quantity of money can no more increase the commodities whose value it is used to measure, than an alteration of the unit

standard measure of length, etc., could alter the quantity of the cloth or other commodities they measure.

154. Let us suppose that every individual in any country should, on rising one morning, find every dollar of money he possessed turned into two dollars,* the first effect would be that all prices would be doubled; but as gold and silver are commodities which the people of all countries are willing to receive in exchange for the articles they produce, the people of other countries would hasten to export their commodities to the country where the increase of gold had taken place and take gold in exchange, until prices, in the country where the increase had taken place, had fallen to their normal state; so that in the case supposed, the increase of gold, having increased the purchasing power of the country, would have led to an actual increase in the wealth of the community.

155. Had, however, the country where the increase of gold had taken place, been shut out from intercourse with other countries, the only effect of the increase of gold would have been to increase the price of all commodities, *and that all debtors would*

* Note well the hypothesis. The money is to be doubled— nothing else, and credit is left out of consideration.

be able to satisfy their debts with a quantity of gold having only half its former purchasing power, while the creditor would receive the AMOUNT *of gold or silver, but only half the* VALUE *he expected.*

If such an accident as the doubling of the money of a country could be supposed to happen as a freak of nature no *wrong* would be committed, although suffering and hardship would result from this transfer to the debtor of a command over the stock of wealth of the community, which the debtor and creditor had alike calculated upon the creditor's receiving; a transfer none the less real because effected by the accidental reduction of the debt, which, remaining the same in name, weight and quality of the coin in which it was to be discharged, is suddenly reduced to half its purchasing power.

156. But if instead of every dollar in the country being doubled, the Legislature were to decree that thenceforth the dollar should contain but half its former weight of gold, and should be received by every creditor in payment of his debt at the rate of one debased dollar for each dollar due, it is obvious that an act of real spoliation would be committed. Various governments have at different times had recourse to this expedient. Not daring wholly to repudiate their debts, they have pretended to pay

them by giving the name of the unit standard of the money in which they had agreed to pay their creditors to some less valuable thing, defrauding their creditors with a high hand, while pretending to pay them. But by thus tampering with the currency, preserving the name of the recognized measure of value while that to which the name has been given is altered, all contracts are violated, and all industrial arrangements disturbed.

CHAPTER XI.

PRICE.   FLUCTUATIONS.   WARNING FURNISHED BY RISE IN PRICE.

157. Price.—Having examined some of the general uses and functions of money, we are now prepared to understand the meaning and effect of fluctuations in price.

Value, as before stated, means the quality of being able to be exchanged for some other commodity or service and is measured by the quantity of commodities or services which can be obtained for the commodity whose value is in question; when the value so obtained is received or measured in money, the term PRICE is employed to designate it; in other words, the value of any commodity measured in money is termed its price.

158. Suppose a cold, wet spring prevailing over Europe to give ground for fearing a deficient harvest in that part of the habitable globe.

Merchants, desirous of earning profit by supplying the most pressing needs of society, endeavor to buy up the stocks on hand in order to withdraw them from the market for the present. Farmers withhold a portion of their stocks, millers and bakers are eager to add to theirs; the prices of breadstuffs rise,—warning the people of Europe to diminish their consumption, and giving notice to the farmers and speculators of America to send all the grain and flour they can spare to supply the needs of the people of Europe. The fears for the grain aroused by the unfavorable spring are followed by fears for the potato in which the blight has shown and begun to spread. Prices rise yet higher. The cold, wet spring is followed by continued rains in June and July. The worst fears for the harvest in Europe are realized, and wheat rises in London to (say) $4.00 a bushel.

Meanwhile America, Russia and Egypt have

been economizing their consumption and hastening forward their stores. Immense quantities are on the way, the risk of famine is over, prices have reached their highest, but care continues to be used in the consumption of the stores on hand until a slight fall in prices proclaims the arrival of the first of the fresh supplies. Farmers, merchants and speculators begin to bring to market the stores they had kept back or accumulated, and realize in profit their reward for the great services they had rendered to society. The telegraph continues to flash tidings of enormous supplies being on the road attracted from all parts of the world by the high prices which have prevailed. Farmers and speculators hasten to bring their stores to market, so as not to be caught with heavy stocks on hand in the face of the increased supplies. Millers and bakers hold back and reduce their stocks to the lowest possible point, in order that they may be able to purchase of the coming store at lower prices. Prices fall; giving notice to distant peoples that the needs of Europe have been supplied and that they may send their grain to countries where it is more needed.

159. Similar illustrations may be drawn from nearly every want of society, and it will be readily perceived that *periods of scarcity must be periods·of*

comparative privation. The rise in price is not the cause, but the effect, first of the anticipation of scarcity, and then of the actual scarcity itself. It is a warning note for diminished consumption, a clarion sound of invitation to distant peoples to supply a scarcity which only this rise in price prevents from becoming a famine.

160. The successful speculator confers a boon upon society which the profit he realizes measures and rewards. They, on the other hand, who, through error in judgment, and sometimes in feeling, buy at a higher price and sell at a lower, withdraw a commodity from market where and when it is much needed, and supply it to one where and when it is less or little needed, and their loss is in general a measure of the injury they have inflicted on society.

161. Here then we perceive another of those harmonies of nature to which we have before referred. *In proportion as merchants and traders benefit or injure society, in that same degree are they rewarded with profit or punished by loss.*

Thus, all the skill, knowledge and judgment of those engaged in mercantile pursuits, while working for their own self-interest, are at the same time enlisted in the service of the community, helping to guard it against want, and supplying what it needs

at the times and places it most needs it, as a means
of earning profit for themselves.

162. Among all civilized communities, the average
prices of imported commodities must be above the
average prices of the same commodities in the countries from which they are exported; and whether
gold or silver flow into or out of a country is a matter of no more importance to the community than
the flowing in or flowing out of the like value of any
other commodity; and were it not the fact that any
given quantity of gold or silver represents an order
on the world's stores for a like value of commodities
deliverable on demand, their export or import would
be of even less importance.

CHAPTER XII.

STRIKES. COMBINATIONS AND LOCK-OUTS. THE PURCHASE POWER
OF WAGES, NOT THEIR AMOUNT IN MONEY, THE PROPER SUBJECT
FOR THE LABORER'S CONSIDERATION. REDUCTION OF HOURS OF
LABOR. TRADES UNIONS. COMBINATIONS TO KEEP DOWN WAGES.
"CO-OPERATIVE" STORES, FACTORIES, ETC.

163. *Strikes and Combinations.*—The student of these pages has already realized to himself

the truth that, whether as capitalist or laborer, the thought which should occupy his mind is not "How "much money am I to get as profit or wages?" but, "What quantity of the necessaries and comforts of "life shall I be able to get for the money I receive "as profit or wages?"

It is unquestionably desirable that this quantity should be a large one, and recourse is sometimes had to strikes and combinations among the employed, and to combinations and lock-outs among employers with a view to increase wages or profits respectively.

164. Let us now enquire whether either or any of these means are adapted to secure the end in view.

We have already seen a very sure course, by which both profits and wages may be increased, viz. : by the general prevalence and exercise, on the part of the administrators of capital, of those qualities which enable them to direct labor to most advantage; and the prevalence and exercise, on the part of the laborers of those qualities which will render their labor most productive and therefore sought after.

165. When the attainment of increased wages and profits is sought through improvement in these qualities, the sympathy conceded to the objects of laborers and capitalists, viz. : increased wages and profits, is granted in even a larger degree to the

means employed to attain them. How is it when recourse is had to *combination?*

166. By combination, in the sense in which it is now used, is meant an organization, composed either of employers or employed, by which, in the one case, a mutual agreement is come to by several employ-ers, to refuse to employ their capital in the purchase of labor, unless the sellers will agree to certain terms proposed by the employers; in the other case it is a like agreement among the sellers of labor to refuse to sell it unless the employers agree to conditions proposed by the employed.

167. As no agreement can be necessary to ensure the performance of, or abstinence from the acts in question, if such acts, or the abstaining from them would be beneficial to those who perform them, such combinations must have for their object to induce or compel those joining in them, *or others* to do that, which in their opinion is injurious to them. As the consequence of men's acts fall primarily upon them-selves, no one can have so sensitive an interest in what he does, as each man himself. To require him therefore, to do what he believes will be an in-jury to himself or those dear to him, is one of the worst forms of tyranny. Nor can we fail to be im-pressed with the contrast which on the one hand

such an antagonism presents between the supposed interests of the various classes of the employed, and between employers and employed generally, to that harmony of their real interests, we, on the other hand have heretofore observed. As truth cannot be inconsistent with itself, this contrast affords an additional incentive to our efforts, to detect the cause of this apparent contradiction.

168. Let us first consider the effect of a combination among the employed to obtain higher wages; If the object be to obtain higher wages for *all* laborers, how is it to be effected? Can the capital out of which wages are paid, be increased at pleasure? By rendering their labor more productive, laborers may induce capitalists to employ as capital, wealth, which would otherwise have lain idle, or been reserved for enjoyment. By this indeed the fund to be divided among laborers as wages would be increased; but what combination to raise wages, by giving to the capitalist a *less* return for his capital, can induce him to convert his unemployed wealth into capital?

But now suppose the combination to be confined to the object of obtaining higher wages, for the laborers engaged in a particular trade. Either the laborers in that trade had been receiving wages lower than what was being paid for the like

labor and skill in other trades or they were not.
If they had, by some of their number transferring
their labor to such better paid trades, or by the natural flow of capital, to the trade in which it was receiving more than the average rate of profit, the desired object would have been obtained, without any
combination to secure it. If on the other hand, the
laborers had been receiving the same reward for
their labor as was then paid for like labor and skill
in other departments of industry, their success in
obtaining increased wages would have the effect of
attracting other laborers from other trades, or of
driving capital from their own, until their wages
had fallen to the general level.

169. Let us now suppose that, the combination
having failed, recourse is had to a strike: that is, a
number of workmen simultaneously cease working,
and refuse to sell their labor, except at an increased
money rate of wages. As we saw in the case of a
combination, if they had been receiving a lower reward for their labor than was being paid for like
skill and labor in equally desirable trades, the strike
was unnecessary because the natural flow of labor
and capital would have produced the desired result,
whereas by ceasing to labor, and yet continuing to
consume, production and capital are diminished; and

while they deprive themselves of present wages altogether, their own future wages and the average wages of all laborers, must fall.

The diminution of production lessens the stock to be exchanged by means of money, and therefore causes prices to rise. The rise in price in the trade in which the strike occurs, necessitates a rise in money wages in other trades, in order that the laborers therein may be placed on an equal footing, thus the prices of all commodities are enhanced, leaving the laborers,—(supposing their strike to have been most successful,) in their former position, *minus* their losses during the strike ; but permanently injured by the bad qualities acquired or the good ones weakened during its continuance.

170. This is by no means the whole of the mischief ; a repetition of strikes has the effect of diminishing the inclination of capitalists to embark in a trade where their reasonable expectations of profit are liable to be destroyed by conduct on the part of others which they can neither direct nor control. Hence diminished capital will be employed in that trade ; from this cause also wages must fall in it, even below the level of other trades, since capitalists will require a larger share of the joint product of the labor and capital employed, to compensate them for the additional risk. 5

171. The remote effects of a strike, especially if apparently successful, are unfortunately generally hidden from the observation of the laborer by the use of money. It will therefore be useful to renew our examination from another point of view.

172. Suppose a strike amongst shoemakers to have resulted in raising their wages from $3.00 to $3.50 per day. Shall the wages of the tailor, who purchases the shoes of the shoemaker, remain the same as before? Not only would it be unjust, but the shoemaker would refuse to consent to it. If, before the strike, two pairs of shoes were worth and would exchange for one pair of pants, the tailor would require such a rise in his wages as should still enable him to obtain two pairs of shoes for one pair of pants. So with the butcher, the baker, the mason, bricklayer, farm laborer, and so through every industrial occupation, until the $3.50 of the shoemaker would procure no more of the necessaries and comforts of life than the $3.00 had previously done.

173. Further, when prices rise, the price of the whole existing stock, which had been produced under low prices, augments and gives to its owners the amount of this rise; adds it in fact to their share of the products of past labor at the expense of those who

have to purchase or hire it from them. Hence, for instance, a strike in the building trade, adds to the wealth of the owners of houses already built; a strike among factory hands to that of the owners of cotton, &c. In the meanwhile, what compensation can the laborer find for his self-imposed idleness of greater or less duration? Let us suppose the number of bricklayers and masons on strike to be three thousand, that their wages were $4.00 per day, and the strike to last twelve weeks, or say seventy working days. In wages alone this represents a loss to the working men of $840,000.00, besides at least double that amount lost to other laborers who depend upon the employment of the bricklayers and masons for opportunities to sell their labor. What quantity of improved houses, what opportunity for a provision against sickness and old age has here been squandered! Even if a rise of say fifty cents a day were a real one, and not as we have seen purely imaginary, it would require to be continued without any interruption of employment for a period of 8 times 70, or 560 working days, (of which for bricklayers and masons there are rarely more than two hundred in a year,) before the loss occasioned by this single, and apparently successful strike could be made good to the strikers.

174. Now let us suppose the object of the strike to be a reduction of the hours of labor.

Let it be assumed that the productiveness of labor in this country is such, that eight hours labor ought to suffice to procure an ample supply of the necessaries and comforts of life to the laborer. That a reduction in the hours of labor ought not to be sought by a strike must be manifest from what has preceded, and that, if eight hours' labor would produce sufficient for the laborer now, ten hours might be necessary after a strike..

175. Continuous labor.—There is, however, an arrangement possible between employers and employed which would be highly beneficial to both parties and which is already generally adopted in most mining industries, viz., that of continuous labor, the workmen being divided into gangs or shifts, which relieve one another.

176. That this is the true interest of the laborer will be apparent from the following* illustration :

The cost of production in say a manufacturing industry is composed of

(1.) Interest and insurance on capital invested in land, buildings and machinery.

---

* The demonstration in the text is taken from an article by Mr. Chas. Moran of New York, which appeared in the *Commercial Advertiser* of New York in December, 1866.

(2.) Wear and tear of tools and machinery.

(3.) Cost of raw material.

(4.) Cost of superintendence.

(5.) Wages.

Of these the first remains the same whether the machinery run six hours or twenty-four.

The second varies nearly in proportion to the production.

The third varies with the production, perhaps a little in excess by reason of some additional waste unavoidable in the case of night work.

The fourth is but little greater if the machinery run twenty-four hours than if it run but six.

The fifth varies in proportion to the production, and loses or gains the whole of the diminished or additional cost of the greater or less quantity of raw material consumed, of superintendence and of wear and tear consequent on the less or greater number of hours the machinery is run.

Capital in the form first mentioned contributes no more to production when a mill runs twenty-four hours, than when it runs six, consequently the remuneration for its risk is neither greater nor less in one case than in the other. Hence labor if not the only, is by far the chief gainer by the additional production consequent on running machinery addi-

tional hours. Let us suppose a cotton mill employing one hundred hands producing 5,000 yards of
cotton cloth daily, running 12 hours, and that under
these circumstances the division of this product
which the laws of supply and demand have established is, one-third to capital, one-third for cost of
raw material and wear and tear, and one-third for
labor.

The mill will produce 2,500 yards when running
6 hours, 4,167 yards when running ten hours, 5,000
yards in twelve hours, and 10,000 yards when running twenty-four hours.

The proportion accruing to capital in each case is
1,667 yards. The proportion to cover the cost of
raw material and of wear and tear in each case will
be 833, 1,111, 1,389, 1,667 and 3,333 yards respectively leaving for labor nothing in the first case 555
yards, in the second 1,111 yards in the third 1,667
in the fourth and 5,000 yards when running twenty-
four hours.

But as a mill requiring 100 hands for 12 hours
work would require 200 for 24 hours we should have
in the latter case double the number of hands employed, each earning twenty-five yards instead of
16,67.

If now the hours of labor be reduced to eight per

day, on the hypothesis that such is the productiveness of labor that eight hours ought to suffice to procure for the laborer a sufficiency of necessaries and comforts of life, the return of each laborer is reduced to 5.5 yards. Run the mill twenty-four hours by three shifts or gangs, thus employing three hundred hands instead of one hundred, and each laborer will receive 16.67 yards in place of 5.5. In other words, eight hours labor will give to each of three hundred laborers by running the mill continuously day and night, the same return which each of one hundred laborers could obtain by laboring twelve hours when the mills run only that time each day, or eight hours labor in the former case will be as productive as twelve hours in the latter.

177. Trades Unions.—A passing glance at those deplorable instances of the submisson of the skilled and industrious mechanic to the will of the idle and unskilled in the operations of Trades Unions, is all that can now be necessary to awaken the attention of the student to the pernicious effects of these organizations as at present constituted.

178. That the managers of these Unions are possessed of great powers of organization is evident. What untold benefits could not result from society and, above all, to the laborers if such power were

employed in the administration of the means at their disposal to useful purposes !

When in spite of the tyrannical restrictions, which these Unions impose upon the peaceful prosecution of industrial occupations by economical, skillful, laborious, and well disposed persons, a store has been accumulated, instead of preserving it for future needs, and increasing it by judicious management, we see the leaders of the Unions wasting that store, by forcing their misguided followers, to days and weeks of idleness, an idleness more or less prolonged in proportion generally, to the amount of savings in hand.

Examine the rules of such societies. They invariably contain provisions, directed to the destruction of all efforts at improvement. Among the bricklayers, the workman is forbidden to lay the trowel out of the right hand while at work, because if he did he could soon work better or more quickly than before. All the Unions require their members to refuse to work in a shop where men who are not members of a Union are employed. No rule is more universal among the Unions or more insisted on by its managers than this, and yet, what decree could be more despotic, what tyrant ever imposed a more galling yoke upon those subject to his will!

179. The case of combinations among capitalists may be readily disposed of.

A general combination of capitalists to keep down wages, is so evidently absurd a supposition, that its mere statement carries with it its own refutation. It means a general combination to destroy capital. Of course if such a thing were possible, wages would disappear along with that capital, which is labor's best friend. A general combination of capitalists to lower or keep down wages, and yet not destroy their capital, is simply impossible. An analysis of the supposition, absurd as it is, will be a useful excercise for the student, and not beyond the powers of one who has read the foregoing pages with attention.

A combination has frequently been attempted among capilalists to keep down the wages of workmen, in a particular trade. The result has invariably been, as the student is now able to perceive it could not fail to be, the partial or total loss of the capital of the men who were so foolish as to engage in it.

180. Co-operative stores, factories and workshops.—Many efforts have from time to time been made to establish various industries, on what have been termed "Co-operative principles." The 'Rochdale Co-operative store' of Rochdale, England

5*

was the first instance of any great success in this direction; a few other cases of successful management have occurred, but the vast majority of such attempts have resulted in loss and dissappointment to all concerned. The causes of the success in the one case, and of failure in the other, will not be difficult to find; but before seeking them, it is desirable to remove an ambiguity resulting from the use of the term "Co-operative;" as though co-operation were peculiar to the industrial arrangements in question.

181. Co-operation.—The student of these pages must have observed that from the moment that the division of labor is introduced into the industrial pursuits of any community, *all who labor co-poerate with one another.*

The shoemaker *co-operates* with the builders of the railroad, and of the steam engine, with the banker and with the farmer; he *co-operates* with the miller to grind flour, with the stockman to breed sheep, cattle and horses, with the mill owner and factory hand to spin yarn and weave cloth, with the tailor to make clothes ; also to invent the printing press, the sewing machine and the electric telegraph, while each and all of the persons engaged in these vocations *co-operate* to produce leather and to make shoes.

So far then as .the term " Co-operative store"
or " Co-operative factory " is intended to intimate
that "*co-operation*" is a feature special, or peculiar,
to that store or factory, the term is a misleading one;
at the same time there is an idea underlying this
ambiguous expression, which is intended to be expressed by it, and what that idea is, it is desirable
clearly to ascertain.

182. Co-operative shops.—In a so-called
" co-operative" shop or factory, the idea intended
to be conveyed is, that those who sell their labor
shall have part of the reward of their labor paid out
of, and be a proportionate share in, the PROFITS to
be thereafter received upon the capital, skill and
labor employed in such shop or factory. This
part then of the wages of labor in "co-operative "
factories or shops is contingent upon profits, increases as profits increase, decreases and disappears
as profits fall or disappear. As an interest in the
future success of an industrial enterprise, is a powerful incentive to honest and earnest labor, *any system or organization which shall give such interest, without diminishing the unity so essential to successful management, must secure to the enterprise organized on such
system, an immense superiority over those in which no
such interest is secured.*

The great difficulty lies in combining, the re-
serving of such interest to them who sell their
labor, with unimpaired efficiency in management.
All attempts in this direction are social experiments, as important steps to progress in
industrial science as experiments in other sciences
have proved to progress in those sciences. Unhappily, in social and industrial science, experience
so derived is generally purchased at a far greater
cost of happiness on the part of the experimenters
than in the case of experiments in other sciences,
nevertheless such experiments furnish important gains
to scientific knowledge, and from out of them in the
course of time will be evolved a real and permanent
gain to industrial organization and social science.

183. The most successful efforts to combine the
two features above mentioned which have yet been
made, consisted in the setting aside, by the owners
of the capital employed, of a portion of the profits
after paying interest upon the capital, to be divided
among the employés in proportion to the wages
earned by them. Thus: if one workman (A) had
earned $500, and another (B) $400 in say one year,
and the amount to be divided was ten per cent.
upon the whole, A would get $50 and B $40 as
their respective dividends.

Some experiments of this kind so far as known have been eminently successful, chiefly in consequence of the carefulness to avoid waste, unexampled industry and trustworthiness which were developed in the workmen, so that both capitalists and employés had largely increased returns for their capital and labor.

One of the most successful and interesting of these industrial partnerships, that instituted at the mines of Messrs. Briggs Bros., of Lancashire, England, was forcibly put an end to by the tyranny of a Trades Union to which some of the miners employed by the Messrs. Briggs Bros. happened to belong, and which they had not the manliness to quit when it launched its arrogant and tyrannical decree.

184. Capital furnished by customers of " co-operative " stores.—In the case of " Co-operative " stores an interest in the success of the undertaking is given, not only to the workers but also to all who by purchasing at the store contribute to its success.

As these stores are conducted on the system of cash payments, both in buying and selling, a great part of the remuneration for use and risk of capital, is saved, while in their sales, the economical aspect from which their customers are regarded, (in fact though not in name,) is that of furnishing a portion of the capital for carrying on the business, and the return they get is in fact, (where the busi- is successful,) a very large interest upon the capital so provided.

185. Qualities of the managers of "co- operative" enterprises.—Now when we exam- ine the various cases of success and failure in these "co-operative" enterprises, one feature stands out prominently, and that is, the very remarkable de- gree in which the managers of the successful "co-op- erative" store or factory were endowed with the in- dustrial virtues, *combined with a most unusual amount of love and sympathy for their fellow men,* and of gen- erosity!

The same industrial virtues, could have made them Rothschilds or A. T. Stewarts for wealth; owners of millions, as the well-deserved reward given by society for services rendered through un- flinching honesty, untiring industry, and marvellous skill.

But their great love for and sympathy with their fel- low men, and their abundant generosity, have induced these self-denying managers to divide with their less gifted fellow-workers the reward earned by their pre-eminence in industrial virtues, and none should seek to detract from the admiration excited by the spectacle of so much self-denial.

186. It is nevertheless yet to be determined whether a general prevelance of so large an amount of self-abnegation would really be beneficial to society. It must not be forgotten that of all the wealth acquired by individuals, all that they convert into capital goes instantly to augment the wages fund, and is therefore, (as seen above, §76,) really consumed and enjoyed by those who sell their labor. It is only that portion which is consumed in the individual; (or family,) enjoyment of the owner which does not go to augment the wages fund, and so far as the wealth itself when realized is concerned, the only difference is as to whether the portion thus reserved for enjoyment, shall be reserved for the enjoyment of the few or of the many.

187. Profits of such organizations in reality a gift from the managers.—The powerful inducement furnished to the laborers to render their labor more efficient is what really recommends this special form of " co-operation " where it can be adopted without impairing the efficiency of management. Unfortunately no plan yet devised has recommended itself as presenting these two features combined, except in the presence of those remarkable industrial virtues on the part of managers which render the so-called "profits" of the "co-operative" enterprise *a free gift from those managers,* to those entitled by the rules of the enterprise to share therein, of almost the entire reward due to the former for the exercise of their unusual qualifications and industrial virtues.

CHAPTER XIII.

CREDIT. FACILITATES INTERCHANGE. IMPROPER FOR DOMESTIC EXPENDITURE. CONSEQUENCES OF THE NONFULFILMENT OF ENGAGEMENTS. LAWS FOR THE RECOVERY OF DEBTS, INJURIOUS EFFECTS OF.

188. Credit.—The introduction of a standard measure of value greatly diminished the labor of interchange, but the devising of a means whereby the actual passing of money could be generally dispensed with, was calculated to diminish that labor in a still greater degree.

Such a means could be found so soon as buyers and sellers were able to *trust each other.*

189. Where the same persons buy of and sell to,

and can repose confidence, in each other, the whole of their transactions may be conducted without any money passing, or at most, by small sums to settle balances struck at stated times.

This selling without receiving the money at the time is termed giving CREDIT. So, too, employers and employed give credit to one another. The employer trusts the employé that the labor or time he has purchased will be faithfully performed or employed; the employé trusts the employer that he will punctually pay the wages contracted for.

The merchant who orders his agent to purchase merchandise trusts him to buy as cheap and as well as possible, yet more does he trust him if he pay for the merchandise before receiving it. So, too, the consignor trusts the consignee of goods, and where he receives advances upon them he both gives and receives CREDIT.

190. The full benefits to be derived from the use of credit can only be realized among a people whose moral tone regards the fulfilment of engagements as a sacred duty.

The capitalist who gives but never receives credit, has no precautions to take to be able to fulfil his own engagements. These are already fulfilled, and the comfort and ease of mind which accompany this mode of dealing and the undivided attention he can in consequence give to the other departments of his business, will frequently more than counterbalance the advantages which, even when all calculations have been correctly made, are obtained by the use of borrowed capital.

For the purposes of personal, household, or domestic consumption the giving and taking of credit can scarcely ever be other than most pernicious in its consequences.

191. There are nevertheless instances in which credit may be employed with advantage to all parties with a great saving of labor to the community, and as a means of taking capital from hands incapable of administering it successfully to place it in those which can do so to advantage.

Let us suppose a dealer having a capital worth, say, ten thousand dollars and a ready money trade of, say, five hundred dollars a week, believing he could greatly increase his returns if he could increase his stock.

Proceeding by degrees, he begins by accepting one, or more, month's credit for one thousand dollars and gradually increases his stock to twenty thousand dollars with a credit of ten thousand dollars payable at various times, the latest being, say, six months, while his ready money trade has increased to $1,000 a week; evidently such a trader would be trading within the bounds of prudence.

If in addition to taking credit, he also sells on credit, greater caution is needed in the credit he takes.

192. The giving of credit incautiously even by one who does not himself take credit, is not to be looked upon as a trifling offense. It is placing the means of doing mischief to themselves within the reach of the thoughtless and inexperienced, and giving opportunities for recklessness and dishonesty.

193. Laws for the recovery of debts.—But the tendency of a judicious use of credit to place capital in the hands of those best able to administer it, has been greatly marred by unwise legislation all over the civilized world.

That capital may fall into the hands of those best able to administer it, credit should be given in reliance only on the honesty, industry, judgment, skill, knowledge, and economy of the borrower.

The penalty prescribed by nature for giving credit to the incapable or untrustworthy, *i. e.*, to those who cannot administer capital to advantage, is the loss of the capital so lent, and this penalty, left free to work, would soon confine the recipients of

credit to the honest and capable, with little regard
to their wealth, except where the want of wealth
would betoken either inexperience or the absence of
one or more of the industrial virtues. But most
nations have passed laws for the supposed recovery
of debts from unwilling debtors, and large staffs of
government officers are kept up at enormous cost to
enforce those laws. In vain! The remedy prescribed, the redress promised has everywhere broken
down and proved delusive. A direct discouragement is also given to the industrial virtues by laws
which pretend to enable creditors to recover their
debts from dishonest debtors. In consequence of
such laws, intending lenders look more to the wealth
than to the conduct and character of the borrower,
thus diminishing the demand for honesty, industry,
and general trustworthiness, and tending to place
capital in the hands of those who may squander
alike their own capital and that which they have
borrowed.

CHAPTER XIV.

BILLS OF EXCHANGE. P. O. MONEY ORDERS. RATES OF EXCHANGE.
PAR OF EXCHANGE.

194. Bills of Exchange.—Arising out of the use of credit is the ingenious device of Bills of Exchange, believed to have been invented by the Jews in the middle ages.

Being one of the most fertile means of facilitating interchange and rendering labor more· productive their invention and employment confer a vast boon upon society; though unfortunately, through the very greatness of their utility, they are liable to grave abuse.

195. A bill of exchange is a written instrument by which a creditor directs his debtor to pay his debt to a third person named therein. It was invented as a means of settling a distant debt without the actual transmission of money.

196. Suppose that every week commodities to the value of $20,000,000 enter New York from various parts of the world, and that commodities to about the same value quit New York; then, but for the device of bills of exchange, the New York debtors

would have to send $20,000,000 to their creditors, and the New York creditors would have to receive the same amount from their debtors, and $40,000,000 in money would have to be sent to and from New York every week. To avoid the expense and risk of such transit, and yet adjust the debts of all parties, the New York creditors write orders directed to their debtors requiring them to pay their debts to the creditors of the New York debtors, and these orders they sell to the New York debtors. These orders are bills of exchange.

The person who draws or makes a bill of exchange is termed the drawer, the person in whose favor it is drawn is called the payee, the person on whom it is drawn, *i. e.*, to whom it is directed, is called the drawee, and after he has accepted it, the acceptor; persons into whose hands the bill may have passed previously to its being paid, who write their names on the back, are termed indorsers, each indorser is also an indorsee from the person who indorses it to him, and the person in whose possession the bill is at any given time, is termed the holder or possessor at that time.

Bills drawn on distant places are called foreign bills. Bills drawn upon the same country or state are termed inland bills.

197. The greater the distance of the places between which the commercial intercourse takes place, the greater will be the advantage of employing bills of exchange in lieu of transmitting coin; the greater at the same time is the necessity that the debtors on both sides should be persons of undoubted probity and punctuality.

The two debts intended to be liquidated by the aid of the bill of exchange transmitted in lieu of coin, are neither of them discharged with the bill drawn on the distant or foreign debtor until that bill is paid, and the failure of the acceptor to pay the bill at maturity would render the New York creditor liable to the New York debtor for the face of the bill and interest, as well as for the loss the latter has sustained through sending a bad bill in the place of good money, while the New York debtor, besides the annoyance and possible loss of seeking to recover those amounts from the New York creditor, would have to purchase another bill, or remit money to liquidate his indebtedness.

198. The system of orders known as Post Office money orders for the transference of small sums of money from one place to another through the instrumentality of the Post Office, is, in fact, a system of Bills of Exchange to the payment of which the public faith of the nation is pledged.

199. Bills of Exchange are also frequently employed between persons residing in the same neighborhood. Where A sells goods on credit to B, he frequently draws a bill for the amount which B accepts payable at any agreed future date. A more frequent practice in this country is for B to give his promissory note, *i. e.*, an instrument in writing by which he promises to pay to A or his order the amount of his debt at a given time. A can then transfer this promise either by sale without recourse, or by simple endorsement to a third person. If transferred without recourse, A has no further interest in the bill or note, but if simply endorsed, A is a guarantor of due payment by B to all subsequent holders and endorsers.

Another peculiarly useful function filled by these bills or notes will be seen when we treat of the subject of Banking.

200. Rates of Exchange.—The value of a bill discounted in the place where it is payable, can never exceed the amount expressed on its face; with foreign bills, or bills drawn on distant places, the value may exceed this amount, by an amount not exceeding the cost of transmitting money with which to discharge a debt payable in that place.

The proportion between the amount of money

given for a bill on a foreign or distant place and the amount of its face is called *the rate of exchange.*

When a bill payable at sight or on demand is worth the amount expressed on its face, the rate of exchange is said to be at *par.*

When the amount paid for a bill of exchange in say New York, drawn suppose upon Germany, is more than its face value, or more can be obtained for it than the figure which represents the part of a Dollar into which the Reichsmark can be coined, multiplied by the number of Reichsmarks expressed in the bill, that is when there are more debtors to, than creditors of, Germany in New York, the rate of exchange in the language in use in this country is said to rise, and bills on Germany are at a premium. Conversely, the rate of exchange is said to fall when the amount paid for the bill is less than its amount, and bills on Germany, (for instance) are then said to be at a discount. Thus the rate of exchange is a variation on one side or the other from the par, produced by the state of the payments between the two countries.

201. The par of exchange between this country and any other which has the same commodity as its measure of value is ascertained by a simple rule of three.

6

To ascertain, for instance, the par of exchange between this country and Great Britain the amount of pure gold in the dollar and the pound sterling is first determined viz.: 23:22 grains in the dollar, and 131 grains in the pound*. Then $1: £1: 23:22: 113, or the dollar equals 0.2055 of a pound or 4 shillings and 1.2736 of a penny.

202. The debasement of the coin or other tampering with the currency, as by the fraudulent device of what, to conceal its dishonesty is termed " an inconvertable currency," affects at once the par of exchange with all other countries.

203. The exchange operations between this country and Great Britain are complicated by an absurd practice of calling the dollar equal to 4s. 6d. or 0.225 of the £1, and marking the fluctuations by giving $100 and a variable number of dollars in' addition for every $100 of the suppositious value of 0.225 of a pound, or 4s. 6d. The par with this suppositious dollar or fraction of the pound sterling is thus obtained: 0.2055; 0.225:100:109.5 very nearly. In other words, one hundred conventional dollars or £22 10s. sterling British, is the equivalent of $109.50 of our gold money, very nearly.

---

* These are the weights of pure gold in the dollar and pound sterling respectively. · The copper or other alloy is regarded as of no value.

204. Unfortunately, governments have frequently adopted the practice of debasing the currency. This has been done either by reducing the amount of pure metal in the coin, and attempting to cheat the public by giving to the reduced quantity the same name which had been borne by the old coin, or by the yet graver though more insidious and disguised fraud of a forced paper currency. It therefore becomes necessary to call attention to the fact, that in such cases the real par is altered and becomes the figure which denotes the quantity of the debased coin into which the quantity of gold or silver bullion contained in the unit of the country with which the par is to be ascertained can be coined; or, in the case of a forced paper currency, the real par is a reduction from the old in the exact ratio of the depreciation of the paper currency.

CHAPTER XV.

BANKS AND BANKING.   DEAL IN SECURITY.   DEPOSIT ACCOUNTS.
DRAWING ACCOUNTS.   CLEARING ACCOUNTS.   NATIONAL BANK
ACT.   SAVINGS BANKS.

205. Banking.—Money being adopted as the medium of exchange, all persons need to have some of it at command at all times, to enable them to supply their daily needs, while traders require, in addition, a provision against emergencies which may arise in the course of their business.

The aggregate of these sums, small individually, amount collectively to a large value, which it is desirable to utilize.   So long as the owners are obliged to keep these sums in their stores or dwellings, they are unproductive, and their owners are involved in constant anxiety, and exposed to great risk of loss.

The want for security thus felt, the need of some one to whom these small sums could be confided, with the certainty that they would be forthcoming on demand, gave birth to a class of traders known as bankers.   The commodity in which they deal is SECURITY.

206. The persons who leave their money with

bankers, (called the bankers' customers,) make their daily payments by drafts or checks—*i. e.*, by written orders on the banker, requiring him to pay to the payee's order, or to bearer, the amount specified therein. Every such draft or check is a bill of exchange. The moneys received by the customers of the bank in the course of their business are also lodged or deposited with the banker, and the banker strikes a daily balance of the amounts so deposited and withdrawn. The amount which is then found standing to the credit of his customer on the banker's books is termed the customer's balance. The account thus kept by the banker, upon which the customer draws for his daily wants, is called the customer's *drawing* account. Besides these accounts, it frequently happens that persons receive moneys which they intend to invest when an opportunity occurs, and on which they desire to earn interest in the meantime. These moneys they gladly lend to a banker at interest, and the account thereof kept by the banker is the customer's *deposit* account.

207. The majority of persons desire to maintain their drawing accounts as nearly as possible at the same amount. When the balance of these accounts, in the case of one class of persons, is drawn upon and reduced, it is generally found that those of other

classes are in excess of their usual amounts. Experience thus shows that the passing away of the emergencies or exigencies of one class of a banker's customers, and the preparations they make for meeting future emergencies, generally balance the exceptional withdrawals of others, and the two series of operations amount practically to little more than a transference of credits upon the books of the banker.

It thus came to be perceived that the banker could, with perfect safety to his customers, lend out a large portion of the funds deposited with him, even though repayable by him on demand, and thus obtain a sufficient remuneration for his skill and labor in taking charge of his customers' moneys, without exacting any payment from them for doing so. The difference between a banker and other industrial workers, in the character of debtor, consists in this : what other traders owe their creditors, the latter wish to use ; what the banker owes is what his creditors wish *not* to use. They hope never to have occasion to use it, but desire to be able to do so on the happening of any emergency requiring it.

208. In Chapter XIV. some account was given of foreign and inland bills of exchange. When a merchant, say A, who has sold goods on credit to, say B, perceives an opportunity for renewing his opera-

tion, he takes B's note, or his acceptance to a bill of exchange, to a banker, who, if he approve of the security, purchases or discounts it with part of the funds deposited with him by his customers, giving, or crediting to, A the amount of the bill or note less the discount : *i. e.*, the interest on the face amount of the bill to the day it becomes due is calculated at an agreed rate per cent. and deducted presently from the amount of the bill or note, and credit is given the customer for the balance.

209. It is by discounting commercial bills that the banker is able to obtain interest on a part of the funds deposited with him, and as those bills are to be had of all dates and amounts, he can, by retaining the amounts paid to him day by day, instead of relending, provide against the decrease of his customers' deposits.

210. It is also by discounting commercial bills that the transfer of capital from one trade to another, in accordance with the exigencies of the hour, is temporarily effected, the slack time of one trade being ordinarily that of briskness in some other.

211. Clearing House.—Until a comparatively recent date, each banker in cities used to send out a number of clerks to collect the claims he held against other bankers of his city, such as bills or notes discounted for, or deposited for collection by his customers, which falling due that day had been made payable at some other bank, or of checks or drafts upon some other bank, deposited with him for collection. This practice compelled each banker to keep cash or notes on hand to meet these claims, and he would often have to pay out large sums to a bank against which he had claims to a much larger amount. To prevent this, as also to diminish the risk from robbery and loss, occasioned by sending out these collection clerks, a " Clearing House" has been established in some of the most important commercial centres of the world.

212. This "Clearing House" is an association of bankers, who meet once or twice a day for a mutual cancelling of drafts, in lieu of paying each draft in money.

213. Of all the clearing houses in the world, that of New York is, when the magnitude of its operations is considered, the most perfect in its operation. During the month of June, 1876, the currency clearances amounted to $1,502,674,460.31 ; the daily average was $57,795,171.55 ; and these were effected by an average daily movement of $3,055,708.75. Even of this three millions, little was actually paid. A depository has been established by the Associated

New York banks, with whom most of them make deposits, receiving certificates in exchange, and the balances represented by the above mentioned $3,055,708.75 were mostly settled with these certificates.

Up to the 1st July, 1876, the amount of the trans· actions of the N. Y. clearing house during a period of 22¾ years was $455,979,252,041.58, yet in all this vast dealing no error to the amount of a single cent remained undiscovered or uncorrected for a single day!

214. The New York Clearing House Association is a purely voluntary one, its members have refused to encumber themselves with a charter, there is no human law to which it can be made answerable, but its orders receive implicit obedience, though the severest punishment any bank can sustain at its hands is to be expelled from the clearing house!

The clearing house serves also as a check or tally upon the different bankers' account, very similar to that which a bank exercises for its customers.

215. There has resulted from the clearing house system of New York,—and doubtless from those of other cities,—an advantage little anticipated by its founders.

By the rules of the New York association, each
6*

bank is bound to furnish to the manager a weekly statement of affairs, for publication.

The statement required by the United States to be furnished by the national banks is often untrue; when this is so, the falsehood can rarely be detected until the bubble bursts, and the bank's insolvency is too apparent from other evidences for longer concealment.

The statements furnished by the members of the New York Clearing House Association might also be untrue, but if so, the untruth would be self-detective. But further, the clearing house association furnishes a premonition of any weakness or mismanagement on the part of its members. Suppose the weekly statement to show on the part of any bank a reserve of say $300,000, and that there should be balance debits on the three following days which should exhaust such reserve, if the fourth day should continue to show a debit of say $30,000, it is evident that the bank must, (save in certain cases,) borrow to meet it, evidence, (in all except the . exceptional cases,) of bad management. The committee of the association then visits the bank; if the bank be one which receives frequent remittances from abroad or from foreign banks, the position is a natural, normal, and, most probably, a proper one, in any other case the bank is more or less involved.

If on examining the bank's affairs, it is found to be perfectly solvent, its embarrassment the result only of slight errors of management, assistance will be afforded it; but if insolvent, or hopelessly embarrassed, it will be excluded from the association, and its career of mischief brought to a speedy close.

216. One of the results which have flowed from this almost automatic disclosure of the condition of the various members of the New York Clearing House has been, that no member has ever been a loser, in the slightest degree, by the failure of another of its members.

The members of the clearing house are thus relieved from the perils of a run in the case of the failure of another member, such as generally follows the failure of one bank, upon other banks doing business with it.*

217. How infinitely to be preferred, how much more reliable, is the protection furnished to the com-

---

* The facts given in the text relating to the New York Clearing house, together with much other valuable information, were furnished to the author by Mr. Wm. A. Camp, manager of that admirably conducted institution, to whom the author desires to render his grateful acknowledgements, as well as for the opportunity furnished him on three occasions of witnessing the business of the clearing house while in course of being transacted.

munity against the evils resulting from reckless
banking, by this voluntary organization, than the
Will-o-the-whisp of legislative or government protection!

218. Among the errors into which nearly all governments have fallen has been that of attempting to
control and direct the business of banking.

219. National Bank Act.—In a work so elementary as the present, it would not be desirable to
enter into any detailed account of the National Bank
act of 1863, a bad copy of a bad original, viz.: Peel's
Act regulating banking in England. It will be sufficient to point out the principal objections to it.

(1.) As security for their notes, the banks are required to deposit at Washington, (*i. e.* out of their own
control,) the very securities by the sale of which at
times of need, payment of these notes and of their
other obligations would be possible.

(2.) A fixed percentage is required to be held in
reserve, and no new loans or discounts may be
granted by a bank whose "reserve" has continued
for twelve days below this percentage. Now, as the
only occasion on which, with due regard to the rules
of prudent banking, the reserves would be liable to
fall below this limit are those when, by reason of
the greater or less destruction of private credit,

banking accommodation is in most demand, viz., in commercial crises, the natural cure for crises is denied to the community, and we have in this provision of the law a careful effort to convert every crisis into a panic.

220. It can hardly be necessary to refer particularly to the class of banks called savings banks, they being subject in all particulars to the same natural laws as other banks.

Their accounts, however, partake far more of the nature of *deposit* than of drawing accounts, and both for this reason, as well as on account of the excessive suffering and misery which the failure of such banks occasion, even more care is required to be exercised by the managers of such banks in the loans they grant and in the character of the securities in which they invest the funds entrusted to their care, than in the case of ordinary banks.

221. Carefully managed savings banks perform for small savings the function which ordinary bankers perform for the larger deposits of their customers. The utility of 'the former however extends much further. Many of the amounts deposited with savings banks would undoubtedly have been lost or squandered in the absence of some place of safe deposit, and these banks therefore exert a power-

ful influence in inducing habits of economy and thrift.

222. The amount of *interest* payable on such deposits should bo alwas a minor consideration. *Security* is tho first. It is to the accumlation of his savings, and not to the interest upon them, that the depositor should look for that provision against sickness and old ago which is to prevent his becoming a burden on the community.

· CHAPTER XVI.

INTEREST.   LIMITS TO.   MARKET RATES.   AVERAGE RATES.   USURY LAWS.

113. Interest.—In tho analysis of profit one of its elements was found to bo a reward for past abstinence, or interest. Rates of interest and discount, (which is interest under a particular form,) vary greatly at different times in the same place, and at the same time in different places; it will bo interesting to investigate these phenomena and to ascertain the cause or causes of fluctuation in tho rate of interest.

224. Before entering upon this inquiry, it is necessary to caution the student against confounding capital with money. When *borrowers apply for a loan, what they really seek to borrow is capital ;* and when money is lent to them, the first step to earning a profit is to exchange the money for machinery, labor, or goods. But capital being measured in money, both borrowers and lenders speak of borrowing and lending so much money, and the interest for the use of CAPITAL is often inaccurately called the interest of money.

This error is often carried still further, as, for example, when the rate of interest is high, money is said to be dear even though the prices of commodities were unusually high, in which case money is lower in value than usual. So too the loan or capital market is miscalled the money market, and various other forms of expression involving the same error are in common use.

225. With this caution, let us now suppose that a certain number of persons desirous of lending their capital were to meet a number of others desirous of borrowing, and between them establish a certain rate of interest.

If now the amount of capital desired to be borrowed should remain the same, and the capital the lenders are anxious to lend should increase, the latter will have to offer the increased capital to the borrows at a lower rate of interest, so as to induce the latter to borrow it, or to tempt additional borrowers into the market. In other words, the rate of interest would fall. As those owners of capital who have no means of employing it except on loan, would rather receive a very low rate of interest than none at all, the rate of interest might fall to anything above nothing. If on the other hand, the increase were in the desires of the borrowers while the loanable capital remained the same, the rate of interest would rise. No limit can be fixed to the rate of interest which even honest and solvent traders might be willing to pay, rather than not obtain a loan of capital to enable them to fulfill pressing engagements. But such engagements fulfilled, new ones leading to like consequences would be avoided, because the object of traders entering into engagements is to earn a profit, which object would be disappointed by the payment of unusually high rates of interest.

226. As it is with a view to earning an additional profit, that administrators of capital add to the capital they administer by loans from other capitalists, the interest they will agree to pay for the use of

such capital will be less than the additional profit they expect to earn. If their calculations be correct. the interest will be paid out of such additional pro-. fit. If their calculations prove erroneous, or their engagements imprudently contracted, the interest. will exceed such additional profit, and either diminish the profits they would have earned, or perhaps even encroach upon their own capital. It is thus evident that the *average rate of interest* prevailing in an industrial community *must be less than the average rate of profit.*

227. Hence it is evident that while the market rate of interest is regulated by the equation of the demand to the supply, modified as to each borrower by the nature of the security he is able to offer, and the degree of confidence his character inspires, the *average rate of interest is governed by the average rate of profit.* In this country, where by reason of an indefinite extent of unappropriated land of great fertility, the return to labor and capital is large, the rate of interest must be high; but where, as in most of the countries of Europe, the rate of profit is comparatively low, the rate of interest will be low also. Hence both labor and capital have a constant tendency to flow from Europe to this country. This tendency is checked and weakened, especially as re-

gards capital, by unpunctuality, dishonesty, and other untrustworthiness on the part of the individuals or of the people, and by unwise legislation.

228. The higher rate of wages consequent on the smallness of the population compared with capital invites laborers from Europe, the greater productiveness of their labor here causing also a higher rate of profit, capital is also attracted hither. The mutual striving and competition among the administrators of capital to earn profit, prevents their securing to themselves the whole of the increased return to capital, but compels them to share it with the laborers, with the owners of eligible lands, and with the owners of the capital they borrow, tending to increase the rates of wages, of rents, and of interest, and thus draw further labor and capital to this country. This competition among administrators of capital tends also to place capital in the hands of those who can administer it to the best advantage, because those who can afford to pay the highest rate of interest combined with the best security are they who will be able to obtain the largest share of loanable capital. Their being able to offer the best security and to pay the highest rate of interest, depends on their being able to so administer the borrowed capital as to earn the largest profits, that is, to direct labor most productively.

229. The fresh instance of the harmony of nature here displayed, is constantly being interrupted in many countries by foolish legislation, and in few respects more mischievously than by laws limiting the rate of interest which may be lawfully taken; known as usury laws.

The limit so fixed by law is in all cases somewhat higher than the ordinary rate of interest established by the average rate of profit for ordinary commercial risks in the community where such laws exist. This is evident, because were the lawful rate fixed, below, or even only equal to such rate of profit, it would put an end to all borrowing by law-abiding people, and the law itself would therefore soon be swept away. Being fixed above such ordinary rate, let us suppose a state of things to happen that the number of borrowers, or rather the capital they seek to borrow is largely increased while the loanable capital remains unaltered.

This arises either from a prospect of profit greatly exceeding the ordinary rate, or from a number of traders having miscalculated their prospects and entered into engagements out of proportion to their means to meet them.

In the first case the operation of the law is to prevent these opportunities for earning an unusual profit from being taken advantage of, *i. e.*, to prevent capital from being employed in the most productive channels, and to force it into employment less productive.

In the second case, persons who have engagements to fulfill are forced either to sell property they would have preferred to keep, at a loss greatly exceeding the interest, however high which they might have had to pay for the loan of the capital they need, or to become or declare themselves insolvent, with all the loss and disgrace thereon attendant. Usury laws are thus seen to oppress most those whom they profess to protect!

230. *An analysis of interest* shows it to consist of three elements.

(1.) Reward for the past abstinence exercised by the possessor.

(2.) Reward for the labor of effecting the loan.

(3.) Insurance against the risk incurred of losing the capital.

The first and second fluctuate but slightly, and are governed by the average rate of profit; the third is the element which fluctuates most, as it is governed by all the elements of uncertainty in the transaction, such as the effects of bad laws or bad government, of untrustworthiness, bad judgment, bad harvests, fires, tempests, etc., etc.

CHAPTER XVII.

PAPER MONEY. ADVANTAGES OF. INCONVERTABLE PAPER MONEY. EFFECT OF. DISHONESTY OF. SUPERIOR HONESTY DISPLAYED BY THE FRENCH PEOPLE OVER THOSE OF THE UNITED STATES.

231.Paper money.—The attentive student may perhaps have experienced some surprise, accustomed as he will have been to associate in actual life the idea of money with certain pieces of printed paper, to find we have made so much progress in our investigations into the phenomena of industrial life without making any reference to these pieces of paper which perform so many of the functions of money. It will be remembered, however, that we had made no little progress, before it became necessary to touch upon the subject of money at all, and the time has now come when these pieces of paper, or PAPER MONEY, may justly claim our attention

232. In considering the subject of credit, some instances were noticed in which credit supplied the place of money, economizing its use, and consequently diminishing the demand for it. Among these instances were book-credits, checks, bills and notes. The creditor to whom a check, bill, or note

is given by his debtor, may transfer it to *his* creditor; the latter to another, and so on to any extent; when the single payment by the first debtor to the last holder of the check, bill or note at maturity will extinguish his own debt and those of all of the intermediate debtors. Checks, bills of exchange, and promissory notes are paper money, economizing the use of metallic money, and thereby diminishing the demand for it.

233. There is, however, a kind of paper money in common use, which is more generally associated with the name of paper money than any other.

This paper money is a promissory note payable, not to order, but to bearer on demand, and is called a bank note or bill because generally issued by some banking institution. It's essential features are, 1, A promise to pay, 2, to bearer on demand, 3, a specified weight of gold or silver of given fineness in the form of coin.

234. The dollar is a piece of metal composed of nine-tenths of gold and one-tenth of alloy weighing 25.8 grains; hence a note or bill which promises to pay a given number of dollars, is a promise to pay so many pieces of gold of the mint standard of fineness weighing each 25.8 grains.

235. When the promise thus made is habitually and

faithfully fulfilled, the coin and paper circulate together and are of equal value. They together form what is generally understood by the term currency, or, the currency of the country.

Confidence being established by the habitual and faithful performance of the promises made, the note will generally be preferred to coin, except for the discharge of balances due to foreign countries where the bills or notes are unknown and consequently do not circulate as money.

236. The preference given to the bills or notes is owing to their being less liable to be lost or stolen, or to depreciation in value by loss of weight. Besides that, the labor expended in counting and transporting is greatly lessened, and that of weighing saved altogether.

So long as the paper money is actually exchanged for coin upon demand, its value will always correspond with the amount promised upon its face. So long, too, as its issue is not interfered with by legislative enactments, the quantity in circulation will be exactly what the community needs and no more.

237. There is only one method by which a larger quantity could be forced into circulation, and that is by causing the paper to be *inconvertable* as it is at

present here, and, (though to a less pernicious extent) in France, Austria, Italy and Russia.

238. An inconvertible paper money is one which promises to pay so many dollars, or other denomination of money, but which promise is habitually disregarded by the promiser, while the law not only exonerates him from fulfilling his violated engagement, but compels all creditors to accept these violated promises in discharge of debts owing to them.

239. A spectacle more dishonoring to the intelligence and good faith of the community where it prevails can hardly be conceived, and its demoralizing influence on all classes can generally be traced. But where the party thus violating its engagements is itself a government, shame and indignation must be the feelings of every honest mind able to discern the difference between truth and falsehood.

240. The wrong thus perpetrated bears with especial severity on those who sell their labor, wages being the last to share in the rise in prices which always follows the depreciation of the money of the country.

241. Neither did our legal tender acts give to the Government the resources they were supposed to furnish. The Government wanted, not money, but men, and munitions of war, which it procured

chiefly by means of its promises to pay. The men it hired had to be clothed, fed and educated for soldiers, instead of being engaged in productive employment. If the cost of such clothing, feeding, and education and munitions of war had been met by taxes judiciously levied, the consumption of the community would have been diminished, and all would have borne their fair proportion of the burthen.

But by giving in exchange only Government promises to pay, nearly the whole amount of these supplies was abstracted from the capital of the country, and was thus a tax levied exclusively on those who sell their labor, the amount divisible among them as wages having been diminished by the food, clothing and other necessaries of life supplied to the army and navy, and the quantity of the products of labor given in exchange for the munitions of war.

The holders, too, of these promises to pay have a claim to the extent of their value on the entire production of the country, which must be again taxed for their redemption.

242. Again, we have seen how enormously the productiveness of labor is increased by the division of labor and by interchange, the latter being indispensable on the institution of the former, while whatever facilitates interchange promotes and ex-

7

tends the division of labor. But to tamper with the measure of value is to disturb all industrial arrangements, impede and partially arrest interchange, and consequently diminish the productive powers of labor.

243. Let us now trace the effect of the debasement of the paper money upon the Government in whose supposed interest it was effected.

Let us suppose the Government to issue $300,-000,000 of legal tenders, as ours did, and the value to fall, as was the case, to 35 per cent. of its nominal amount. It is true that in such a case, while the Government remains bound by its promise to pay $300,000,000, it has received for it in commodities only such value as is represented by the value of its promises measured in the metallic standard at the date of each successive issue—i. e., the amount of gold which the depreciated paper will purchase, diminished by the increase in prices occasioned by the general "briskness of trade," and by the anticipation of further depreciation of the paper. This last consideration is of great moment, and has hitherto been unobserved even by writers on the subject, but which we believe really exceeds that of either of the others.

The government which issues promises to pay to bearer, and does *not* pay, thus forfeiting its faith, loses a considerable portion of its credit, the currency depreciating the more there is issued, the government needs to issue more and more with each successive issue, to procure only the same value as before. The temptation to continue such issue is so strong when the broad line of demarcation between good faith and dishonesty is once passed, that contractors with government have to take all these things into consideration, and to demand from the government, prices that shall yield them not merely the ordinary profit on their capital at the augmented rate of prices, but sufficient to compensate them also for the risk incurred lest the promise to pay $1,000 received by them from the government to-day may be worth less than $1,000, by any amount short of the whole, when the government pays them, not in dollars but in further promises to pay, which may have been in the interval yet further depreciated by further issues to any unknown amount. But the governmental loss does not end here; the contractor who finds himself disappointed of his just profits applies himself to outwit the government which has wronged him. He supplies inferior goods in fulfilment of his contracts, and to enable such goods to pass muster, offers temptations to the government officers to violate their duty.

244. The foregoing observations are illustrated and confirmed to a remarkable degree by the modern financial history of our own country. In May, 1862, the depreciatian of the paper money was 3 per cent.; in June, 9 per cent.; in July, 15 per cent.; in September, 22 per cent.; in October, 29 per cent.; in December, 32 per cent.; while in June, 1864, it was 65 per cent.; or, as it was incorrectly called, gold stood at a premium of 185 per cent. In other words, the promise of the United States Government to pay one dallar was valued only at 35 cents, notwithstanding that such promise could be paid away by the holder in discharge of a debt of one dollar, even though his debt might have been contracted by him when the paper dollar was really equal in value to the gold!

245. The continual rise in prices, consequent on over issue, "stimulated trade," and, induced excessive speculation, that is, encouraged the entering into engagements wholly unwarranted by the means possessed by those entering into them. In such a state of things, so long as prices continue to rise all goes well with the speculators, but the moment a stop is put to the printing presses, and means adopted having in view the fulfillment of the promises issued in such profusion by, "contracting the cur-

rency," prices begin to fall. The speculative dealer who had embarked not only his own capital, but all he could borrow of others, first sees his imaginary profits disappear, and according as he misjudges the position or rightly appreciates it, he either endeavors to borrow, at greater and greater sacrifices, on more and more onerous terms, to postpone the evil day of realizing his loss, but finally aggravating it; or if of sounder judgment he realizes at once, and holds his hands from further speculative purchases, knowing that as the process of "contraction," proceeds, prices must continue to fall as measured in a money, the value whereof continues to rise as the time for the redemption of the public faith draws nearer. Hence a general "stagnation of trade," correlative to the former briskness.

246. But as the money rate of wages was the last to follow the general rise in prices and in fact never reached a full commensurate level; so it is either the first to feel the fall, or its rise to the commensurate level is arrested, the stagnation of trade causing laborers to be at once thrown out of employment, and a general and real fall in wages follows. But this stagnation is aggravated by the uncertainty which a constantly varying

measure of values introduces into all industrial arrangements. Prudent persons limit their dealings to strict necessaries ; farmers, mine-owners, manufacturers, stay their production, lest the prices realized should be insufficient to replace the cost of the wages of labor employed in production ; and present suffering is aggravated by the prospect of future want through the comparative arrest of production.

But now healing nature provides the remedy for the evils and suffering resulting from the violation of her laws. The fall in price invites the attention of foreign traders, who may now perhaps repurchase here the very goods they had previously sold as well as our own products, paying for them in coin or gold previously exported, thus smoothing the road to the redemption of the public credit, and bringing to a term the general loss.

247. Pending this process, however, heavy failures occur among those who had speculated beyond their means, often involving in their ruin comparatively innocent and careful traders, distrust more or less general follows, credit and bills of exchange which have enabled so much money to be dispensed with are refused, thus still further reducing the quantity of the measure of value, occasioning a further fall in prices, renewed failures, increased dis-

trust and what is called a *commercial crisis.* The Government is apt to be assailed by the reckless and ignorant or dishonest traders, to save them from the consequences of their own misconduct; and as it was the errors of the Government which first encouraged the excessive speculation, it is found difficult to withstand the outcry of men rendered desperate by their losses, and by the dread of further loss, but still able, if not altogether to control, powerfully to affect elections. The welfare of the great masses of the people, of those who sell their labor, and of the small capitalist, is too apt to be lost sight of, and the suspension of the attempt to re-enter the path of honesty is decreed; or a *paternal* minister of finance steps in and by the re-issue of retired overdue promises to pay, to aid the "moving of the crops," impedes the progress towards redemption and honesty to the discomfiture of honest workers.

248. The currency of the United States, irrespective of commercial paper, may at the present time be regarded as consisting of three kinds :

(1.) The gold dollar, used in all foreign exchanges, and in some instances of domestic trade.

(2.) The United States legal tenders, or Treasury notes, commonly called greenbacks, as also the fractional currency; for so great was the depreciation of the currency, that even copper cents became more valuable as copper than as coin, and were either melted down or hoarded ;—

(3.) The new "trade dollar" and silver currency marking fractional parts of the greenback "dollar ;" and

(4.) The National bank currency.

249. No effort should be spared for the redemption of the National faith.

The course which has been adopted by the French since the close of their causeless and disastrous war with Prussia, reflects as much credit upon them as by contrast it serves to exhibit in more glaring colors the extent of our errors.

Falling, at an early stage of the war, into the same error which was committed by our Government, at the first moment of peace, measures were inaugurated having in view the redemption of the public faith, and notwithstanding the enormous cost of the war, and of the fine exacted by Germany, they have taken such effectual steps towards resumption, that the depreciation of their currency has disappeared.

This has been done under difficulties compared with which ours have been as nothing, while they have enjoyed but few such magnificent resources as those with which nature has blest this country and people.

250. Besides redeeming the national faith, all interference, whether by the National or by State governments, with the business of banking, as with other trades, should be absolutely prohibited.

Our own financial and banking history is fraught with illustrations of the pernicious consequences of government interference, and the benefits which flow immediately upon its cessation or diminution.

CHAPTER XVIII.

COMMERCIAL CRISES AND PANICS. THEIR CAUSES. AGGRAVATED BY USURY LAWS AND GOVERNMENT INTERFERENCE. HOW TO BE PREVENTED.

251. Crises and Panics.—When a large number of persons are unable to pay their debts, and a still larger number have great difficulty in doing so, a state of things exists in the loan or capital market to which the term CRISIS or COMMERCIAL CRISIS is applied. When the number of those who are unable to fulfill their engagements is so large that credit almost disappears and confidence is replaced by an almost universal mistrust, then a PANIC is said to exist.

7*

If all persons observed the rule evolved in Chapter XIII., of never accepting credit save when they possessed a reasonable prospect of discharging their obligations at the time appointed, neither crisis nor panic could occur.

252. If now we suppose merchants, manufacturers, and bankers to have taken credit, and either from want of judgment or unscrupulousness in undertaking engagements, or from mismanagement of the means at their disposal, to be unable to fulfill all their engagements; loss is inflicted on all who trusted them, laborers and other persons in their employ are discharged, and frequently suffer great deprivations while the failure of a bank entails so much loss and confusion upon its customers as generally to occasion also the failure of all but the very prudent and cautious among them.

When, in addition, engagements have been entered into for the supply of capital for joint stock enterprises, such as the construction of railroads, bridges, ships, docks, piers, warehouses, and the like, not only may these operations be arrested but the contractor for them may be ruined and the laborers he employed be also displaced.

253. The liability to be thus displaced furnishes a fresh reason for economy on the part of the labor-

ers, in order that the industrial derangement in which they may thus chance to be entangled may neither find nor leave them destitute of resources.

254. Such failures as above mentioned always involve the dishonor of bills of exchange, and promissory notes, and as it is chiefly in the purchase or discount of these securities that the loan market is engaged, the consequences of a single failure up to a general suspension of payment should be inquired into.

255. A single failure, unless of great magnitude, does not effect very much mischief. The immediate creditors of the insolvent suffer loss, but it falls within the margin allowed for by the lenders of capital. It diminishes their profits and consequently lessens the return to labor and productiveness of it. It tends to diminish confidence and lower the general tone of morality, but there the mischief ends. If the failure is on a large scale, or failures are numerous and in rapid succession, a general want of confidence is produced. Capitalists hesitate more than ever whom to trust; and they who depend upon the opportunities for borrowing which they had previously enjoyed for the means of fulfilling their engagements, are generally obliged to stop payment.

256. An illustration of the rise and progress of a commeacial crisis will render the cause of these industrial disturbances more apparent.

Let us suppose the stock of cotton cloth had been considerably diminished, and that some New York merchants observing the fact, had contracted with some mill owners of New England for all the cotton cloth which the means and credit at their command would enable them to purchase.

They sell these goods at a large profit and immediately repeat their orders. Other capitalists observing their success, imitate them, and orders pour into New England faster than the mills in operation can supply them.

To pay for the goods thus ordered, the merchants embark all the money and pledge all the credit they can command. So long as the orders are unexecuted, so long that is, as the supply continues low, the increased orders lead to enhanced prices, and all goes merrily along. But in their eagerness for profit, the merchants have noticed only the rise in prices and failed to notice the immense increase in orders and manufacturing appliances. The goods arrive, and what is called a "glut" is found in the market. The expected profits disappear, and prices fall to such a level that the sale of the goods fails to provide funds even to meet the engagements entered into. At this time we shall be told there is "a tightness in the money market" and an additional issue of legal tenders will be clamored for; or the banks will be upbraided for extortion or usury because (where the law has not unwisely interfered to prevent their so doing,) they seek to arrest the evil by refusing to lend except at such rates of interest as shall afford them an insurance against the increased risk of loss which has grown out of or been consequent upon unsafe trading, and shall at the same time diminish or limit the demand for capital, to an equation with the supply.

257. When the legislature has been guilty of the folly of depriving commerce of one of its chief natural indicators of impending disaster, (as by limiting the rate of interest to be lawfully taken,) the banks are compelled to protect themselves by a more peremptory limitation of their loans, the law thus depriving the banks of their insurance, and the public of that bank aid which would prevent a crisis from becoming a panic.

258. The entering into transactions out of proportion to the capital possessed by the speculators is now seen to be the prime cause of a CRISIS.

Legislative interference with the rate of interest or with the business of banking, as in the United States and in Great Britain, is the cause which most frequently converts a crisis into a panic, though a wide spread prevalence of the overtrading above illustrated, might be sufficient to occasion it even in the absence of such legislation.

259. The destruction of credit has a two-fold effect upon the currency, it diminishes the supply of the substitutes for money and increases the demand for it.

That portion of credit such as bills of exchange, promissory notes, and cross accounts, which were really substitutes for money, having disappeared, the supply of money is in effect diminished. Further, the disappearance of that portion of credit which postponed the demand by "changing the office of money "from that of transferring the ownership of the pro- "perty or commodities sold to that of liquidating the "obligations which represent them" causes a demand, which would have existed in the future only, to be immediate and pressing. Hence a sudden and enormous fall in prices.

260. It is at such times that the evils of legislative interference are most severely felt. One of the chief substitutes for money,—credit, — at least private credit, being in a great ·measure annihilated, the

banks are the only available resource, and their issues should now be largely increased through the
liberal discounting of well secured commercial
paper limited by charging high rates of interest.
This is forbidden to the banks in many of the
States by usury laws, while in the case of the national banks such aid is prohibited by the laws as
to their reserves, which compel the banks to restrict
their loans at the very times they are most needed
by the public.

261. The conclusions to which we are forced are,
that *commercial crises have for their sole cause the
abuse of credit resulting from ignorance and want of
honesty, and the evils of this abuse of credit are intensi-
fied by legislative interference.*

262. The remedy is apparent; good teaching and
training in youth in order that honesty, knowledge,
and skill may take the place of dishonesty and ignorance among traders, and that enlightened legislators
may undo the follies of their predecessors.

Of this, good teaching, instruction in the conditions of human well-being and in the phenomena of
social and industrial life is an essential element.

CHAPTER XIX.

FOREIGN COMMERCE. PROTECTION TO NATIVE INDUSTRY. "PAU-
PER LABOR OF EUROPE" CONSIDERED. EVIL RESULTS OF THE
TARIFF ON NATIVE INDUSTRY.

263. Foreign commerce.—The harmonies
which have been seen to exist between the interests
of each individual and of society have developed in
proportion as man was left free to seek his own welfare in his own way. Instances have occurred and
been examined in which the action of the legislature has interfered with such liberty under the impression or pretence that the legislature could more
wisely direct man's efforts for his well being than he
could himself. So far as we have examined such
cases, the results of all such legislative action has
been most pernicious, arresting the progress of production,—forcing labor from more productive channels of employment into such as are less so, aggravating periods of deprivation or of diminished enjoyment into positive distress, scarcity into famine, and commercial crises into panics. The actual
state of our civilization renders it necessary to examine the effects of legislative interference in another direction from those hitherto investigated.

264. In the growth and progress of the division of labor different industries were found to be best adapted to different countries and to different parts of the same country the inhabitants whereof devoted themselves to the production of the commodity for which they possessed special facilities as the readiest means of obtaining the other things they desired. Labor being thus rendered more productive the enjoyments of all were increased. The distances between the producers and the consumers of the various articles, and the cost of transport of commodities from the places of production to the places of consumption formed serious drawbacks to this distribution of industry, which only the immense increase to the productiveness of labor occasioned by it, could overcome.

265. These drawbacks have been sought to be diminished by improving the means of intercommunication.

Not to mention the earliest stages of progress,— turnpike roads superseded the old highways, clipper-built ships took the place of Dutch and Spanish galleons, and finally the locomotive and the steam vessel have almost supplanted the turnpike and the sailing ship, while the electric telegraph instantaneously communicates the wants and desires of one part of the globe to another, adding enormously to the productiveness of men's labor.

266. For anything that has thus far appeared, the division of labor and the interchange of commodities are not more to the interest of one people or class of producers than to that of any other.

The interests of California, have in this respect at least, seemed to be identical with those of Mexico ; those of Maine, and Louisiana with those of Lancashire and Yorkshire in England; of Pennsylvania with those of the black country (England), and of Wales ; Nevada with Mexico, Utah, and China with Italy and France. In short, left to the operation of the workings of man's nature, the whole civilized world becomes one country, having harmonious interests, and one common to all, *viz.* : to carry to its furthest possible development the division of labor, and to this end to diminish to the utmost the obstacles to interchange.

267. But with this harmony of nature, the legislatures of various countries have been induced to interfere. Unquestionably, the law of self-preservation is the highest law, and if it can be shown that the welfare of the individuals composing any community requires this legislative interference, all objections to it must disappear so far as regards that particular community.

268. All nations have desired to improve and cheapen the means of communication and of transport :—When by the aid of such improved means of transport, commodities have been brought to the doors of willing purchasers, ought they to be forced by penalties in the shape of customs duties, to purchase in their stead commodities which have been produced at home at a greater cost of labor than was necessary to procure them by exchange ?

269. Such is the question involved in every proposal to impose duties on the importation of foreign produce for the encouragement of home industry.

270 It certainly seems, at first blush, that it would have been far wiser to have abstained from expending so much labor and capital on the making of roads and otherwise facilitating interchange, if when about to use the means thus provided, impediments to their use are to be put in the way. More logical would it be to destroy the railroads, sink the ships, cut the wires of the telegraph, than to suffer them to be used to bring commodities to their destined port and there seek to arrest their entry to the homes of those who desire to enjoy them.

Left to themselves, the directors and administrators of labor and capital, employ that labor and capital in the mode in which they think most likely

to produce the largest profit. As they do this at
their own risk, it is strange that legislators, on
whom devolve none of the responsibilities of failure
or risk of loss, should think that they are benefitting
the community by forcing or inviting the administrators of capital to abandon the path selected by
them as the one in which, in their judgment, most
profit is to be earned, that is in which labor would
be most productively employed, to enter upon
another dictated by the legislature.

271. The nature of the trade between different
countries and between different parts of the same
country, when left to itself, depends upon the relative superiority one locality has over another in some
special branch of industry. This local superiority is
owing, sometimes to differences of soil, climate, mine-
ral productions, or geographical position, sometimes
to differences in the character, temper and education
of the people, sometimes to priority of invention or
investment, sometimes to the density of population ;
or to a combination of any or all of these conditions.

272. In the more densely peopled countries, articles of food and commodities intended to enter into
the manufacture of other commodities and which are
usually termed raw materials, are in general comparatively difficult of production, but are readily and

cheaply transformed into manufactured articles. In the less thickly peopled countries on the other hand, the production of food and raw materials is generally easy, their transformation into manufactured commodities more difficult. Left to themselves the people of this country, except in its more thickly peopled parts would devote themselves mainly to agricultural and mining industries and to the invention and production of labor-saving machines; and with these products of their industry, skill and capital would procure elsewhere most of the manufactured articles they desire. Even in the face of the restrictions and burthens with which Congress has trammelled commerce, this natural course of trade goes on to a very great extent as will be seen at once by examination of the exports and imports of the country during any period of time.

Admitting the government should protect the producer from being compelled to part with the fruits of his industry without obtaining what he desires in exchange, it would be strange, indeed, to conclude that government should under the plea of "protection" impose restraints upon this freedom, and inflict upon him a penalty whenever he sought to exchange his product for certain other commodities

273. The cry for "Protection to native industry" has arisen in this country in this wise.

Some one, the owner suppose of land in Pennsylvania, discovers a vein of rich iron ore running through his land, with seams of coal contiguous thereto. He proposes at once to dig into the earth, extract the ore, roast and smelt it and sell the product.

He finds on calculating the cost of mining, roasting, and smelting the ores and adding thereto the average rate of profit prevailing in Pennsylvania, that by the time he brings it to the shop of the machinist, its cost to him will be higher than that at which iron carried all the way from Great Britain or Sweden is being sold. He goes to Washington and says to Congress, "See! here is iron ore in abundance, but it cannot be worked because owing to the high price of labor, we cannot compete with the pauper labor of Europe; but if you will PROTECT NATIVE INDUSTRY by imposing a duty upon all iron imported, employment will be afforded to a large number of laborers, and we shall be independent of England and her pauper laborers."

274. As the foregoing argument is that which has been and is now actually and repeatedly employed, it is necessary to guard the student against hav-

ing his judgment warped by prejudice. Honest industry must even feel dislike for paupers, even though it may pity them. But the term "pauper labor" is a verbal contradiction like the expression "honest deceit," "pious fraud," and the like, with which judgment is not rarely led captive in the chains of prejudice.

275. Now the first thing which strikes the student in examining this " PROTECTION TO NATIVE INDUSTRY " is, that whereas the farmer had, before the imposition of the tax, produced the iron he required by exchanging his corn for iron from England, Sweden, and Sardinia, he is now forcibly prevented from doing so. If he could have obtained more iron for his corn and flour by exchanging it for iron, mined and smelted here, he would have gladly done so ; he only resorted to foreign iron, because he thereby obtained MORE for his labor embodied in his corn and flour. Has his labor been protected? Has he not on the contrary been deprived of a portion of the produce of his toil, and that portion handed over, *against his will*, to the American iron-master? And has not that iron-master been induced by the tax thus levied upon the rest of the community and handed over to him, to administer his capital in the employment of labor less productively than he would otherwise have

168 COMMON SENSE; OR,

done? When to this is added the taking an army of men from productive employment to be employed as custom house officers, spies, and informers, can we any longer doubt the mischief, loss, and demoralization this supposed "protection" entails upon the community.

The main reason why the iron-master here may not be able to compete with the English or Swedish iron-master is, that owing to the almost boundless extent of fertile land still unappropriated, labor applied to the land in this country is far more productive than when employed in transforming raw materials into manufactured commodities.

276. To talk of the labor of Europe as pauper labor because the toiling millions of Europe are less fortunate in the remuneration they receive for their labor than their co-workers here, is not only unkind; it is *untrue*.

The pauper is one who lives wholly or partly on the industry of others without giving any adequate return; his own labor, if he labor at all, not being sufficiently productive to support him.

The laborers of Europe live on the products of their own industry unsupported by charity or by wealth taken from others. The iron-master of Pennsylvania and the cotton spinner of Lowell, though rolling in wealth, are paupers, because they require a bounty to be paid to them by the community, expressly on the ground, (disguised, it is true, by the use of ambiguous terms,) that their own labor is not sufficiently productive to support them without such tax!

277. The absurdity of the assertion that the civilized farmer of Iowa, Ohio, or Illinois cannot compete with the nearly savage Boer or Kaffir of Africa would be too great to need notice, but for the fact of its being persistently maintained, though also disguised beneath a cloud of words.

Thanks to the advantage afforded him by his climate, the Kaffir raises on the hills of Southern Africa wool which to him is useless. He gladly exchanges it for flour, cheese and other comforts hitherto unknown to him, and which he now begins to look upon as necessaries.

Europe and America take from him the wool, and give him wheat or maize in exchange. In so doing, they obtain for a day's labor on wheat or maize wool which would have cost them from three to fifteen days' labor to produce directly. The savage took a step in civilization and obtained what he could not have raised at all. Ohio, Illinois and Iowa can raise wool, but while, owing to the warmer and

8

dryer climate of South Africa, the sheep raised there need no protection from the weather, in Iowa, Ohio, and Illinois, stalls, pens and other enclosures must be provided for them ; hay and roots must be raised to feed them, anfl a civilized man must spend from two to eight days' labor where the half-savage Kaffir need spend but one. And the civilized man needs to be " protected" against these beginnings of honest industry of the savage !

278. The pretence that " protection" is needed because of the heavy taxation under which a people labors is equally absurd. To increase taxes is certainly an odd way of proceeding to lighten the burthen of taxation. The attempt, by means of a tariff, to throw the burthen upon foreigners, is entirely futile.

279. Suppose that by reason of the tariff it becomes profitable to employ capital and labor in a branch of industry theretofore supplied by importation. On the amount now produced at home no portion of the tariff tax can be paid by the foreigner. Government gets nothing in respect thereof, but the community pays the tax on the entire quantity produced at home, as a bribe to the few persons who embark in the trade to induce them to do so.

Let us now suppose some of the taxed commodities to be imported. The foreigner has the markets of the whole world open to him. He will not consent to sell to the tariff-ridden community cheaper than to any one else. If the previous demand of the country, now punishing itself with a tariff, formed any considerable proportion of the total demand, he would diminish his production of that particular article, disposing of his stock on hand at a cheaper rate to the rest of the world while the tariff-ridden community would pay not less than the reduced price to the importer, plus the total amount of the tax and of the additional expense and labor it occasions. The foreign producer would then direct his labor and capital, set free by reducing his production, into some other channel until, by reason of the diminished supply, prices rise sufficiently to compensate him.

Of the total loss to the commercial world occasioned by the diminished productiveness of labor, the foreigner bears in the long run, that proportion which his purchases from the tariff-ridden community bear to their entire production, leaving them to bear a loss greatly exceeding the entire produce of the tax.

280. It is strange to observe that the cry for "protection" on account of heavy taxation is raised

chiefly against the production of that nation, (England,) which until the recent Franco-Prussian war raised the largest revenue in proportion to her population of any nation in the world.

281. But the cry that "protection" by customs duties is necessary in consequence of the lower wages, lower rents, and lower taxes of other nations implies yet another contradiction. It assumes that the more civilized a people the less they can be trusted by their government with their own concerns, and the less are they able to "compete" with people who are less civilized. If wages are high it must be because labor is highly productive.* If taxes are high among a people who themselves determine the amount of their taxation, it is because the ramifications of the government are greatly extended and the people believe they have an equivalent in efficient protection to person and property, the education of the people and so forth. If, as is most probably the case, this belief is erroneous, the governmental expenditure whether federal, state or local, is, in effect so much taken from the productiveness of labor, the remedy for which is greater enlightment of the people to provoke them to remove the burthen of such taxation. Rents on the other hand can only

---

* *I. e.*, Real wages as distinguished from money wages.

be high where the progress of civilization has permitted the aggregation of a dense population.

282. It is also alleged that by the imposition of the tax upon the imported commodity, say stonewares or iron, employment will be given to a large number of laborers, and it is implied that this is a good thing. It will hardly be contended that to employ a number of laborers to dig holes in the ground and then to fill them up again, would be a good thing, yet the two cases are precisely parallel. The capital which a tax on iron or stoneware imported into this country induces the owners to employ in pottery or iron mining and smelting, must have been transferred from some other employment in which, at least a like number of laborers had been employed, who, by this transfer, lose their occupations. If the loss be spread over the whole body of laborers, wages are diminished. If the capital now bribed to enter into pottery, iron-mining or smelting, were not so employed, it would seek employment elsewhere, and give employment to at least an equal number of laborers or increased wages to others. But further, by the hypothesis, that if left to itself, capital would not seek the "protected trade," *i. e.,* not unless it be "protected," it must be because, in the opinion of those most competent to

judge, the labor it engages and pays would yield a larger return in some other industry. The difference between the yield of labor thus misdirected, and of what it would produce if directed by a capitalist under a system of freedom and individual responsibility, is so much abstracted from the future capital of the country. It is equivalent to a'perpetual tax upon the wages of the present and of every generation of future laborers, *in addition* to the tax paid by the present generation in their character of consumers of the commodity produced at the enhanced cost.

283. Add to all this the cost of officials to collect the duty, to detect smuggling, of the honest laborers lost to the community and converted into criminals by laws which make innocent actions into crimes, the hosts of spies and informers created by such laws, the treachery and mistrust which they reward and disseminate, and astonishment struggles with indignation to see a people so completely masters of their political actions as are the citizens of the United States imposing upon themselves a yoke so grievous and so demoralizing as a Tariff.

284. Some striking illustrations of the heavy burthen upon American industry imposed by this pretended protection have recently fallen under the author's notice.

In order that mining may be conducted with knowledge and skill, frequent assays of the earths met with in sinking a shaft are neecessary;—an assay for gold, silver, lead, or copper in Colorado costs from $2.50 to $5.00, and is so serious a tax upon the miner, that not anything like the number of assays can be afforded by him as ought to be made to guide his labors. In Germany the cost of such assays is 50 pfennings, or 12½ cents.

If it be said the reason of the difference lies in the higher wages of the laborer, the answer is untrue, for though the *money* wages of skilled labor are higher in the United States than in Europe, its *real* wages are lower, in consequence of the tariff. A suit of clothes will cost a skilled artisan in the United States from six to eight days labor. The skilled artisan of Europe will procure the same clothes for from three to four days labor.

Unwise legislation has not yet succeeded in entirely counter-balancing those natural advantages which tend to render labor so much more productive in this country than in Europe, so far as unskilled labor is concerned, and there thus still exists considerabfe inducement for unskilled laborers to flock to our shores.

285. Among the articles employed by the assayer,

the "scorifier" is used in large quantities. These cost in Germany 1½ pfennings each, or 8 for 3 cents. They cost in Denver 3 to 4 cents each. The assayer in Germany never uses the same scorifier twice ; his Colorado brother often does so, at considerable risk of having an inaccurate assay. The duty is 40 per cent. *ad valorem* and 50 cts. per lb, making together, more than 100 per cent.

Common salt is essential to the chlorinization process in the reduction of ores ; its enormous cost, owing to the duty, renders its use on a large scale impracticable.

286. If the duty on articles used in assaying were removed, the cost of an assay might be reduced to about 75 cents to $1. If the duty on all articles used in reducing ores were removed, mines now absolutely worthless would be highly profitable.

287. Quite recently a number of capitalists contemplated the establishment of reducing works in Colorado which would have given employment to about 2,000 men and boys.

On estimating the cost of the necessary plant, machinery, materials, and the *money rate of wages*, it was found that it would be more profitable to ship the ores over 5,500 miles to be treated in Germany !

288. If the duty on plant, machinery and materials

to be used in reducing ores, and upon clothes and other articles to be consumed by the employés in such works were removed, the works would be at once put up, direct employment would be given to 2,000 men and boys in Colorado, and the whole trade and industry of the country would be proportionately stimulated.

289. By the serious fluctuations in price occasioned by the tariff, scarcity, in countries which do not produce grain, is converted into famine. The most striking illustration of this truth is furnished by the too celebrated Irish famine of 1846-7.

But for the tariff-laws which then existed in Great Britain, the markets of the whole world would have been open to, and prepared to supply the failure of the potato crop in Ireland, and no such disaster would have followed as then swept away nearly one-third of the inhabitants of that country, leaving large numbers weakened and diseased to hand down enfeebled frames and sickly constitutions to their offspring.

290. In a table published in "The Exchange," New York, 1870, will be found the highest, lowest, and average prices of breadstuffs in England for each year for the quarter of a century prior and subsequent to the famine, and repeal of the British tariff

8*

on grain. The contrast between the extremes of prices in the former period and the very slight fluctuations of the latter are most striking. Failures of the crops in Great Britain have since occurred to even a greater extent than in 1846-7, producing distress and suffering it is true—but never a famine.

CHAPTER XX.

KNOWLEDGE ACQUIRED BY THE ATTENTIVE STUDENT. HIS FUTURE HAPPINESS DEPENDENT ON HIS OWN CONDUCT. INDIVIDUAL SUCCESS DEPENDENT ON SERVICES RENDERED. CAUSE OF OCCASIONAL EXCEPTIONS. CANON OF GOOD AND EVIL.

291. The student by whom the foregoing pages shall have been studied will be prepared to enter upon the battle of life forewarned of some of the difficulties which have beset his less fortunate predecessors. But he must not suppose he has mastered the science of human well-being. He stands only upon the threshhold of the temple of knowledge, having learned just enough to enable him to penetrate further within her portals.

292. One all important knowledge he will however

have acquired. He cannot fail to have learned that *his future success and happiness will depend on his own efforts and conduct*, and to look upon each instance of failure on his part, as a consequence of some error in judgment or conduct of his own. Happy indeed for him that this is so. His own conduct he will be able to control in the future, and so prevent a recurrence of like failure. Were failure or success dependent, not on one's own conduct, but on that of others, miserable indeed would be the lot of man.

293. Happily the harmonies of social life render individual success dependent on the services rendered by the individual to society at the same time that they leave him master of his own future. Occasional, (and sometimes dazzling,) instances are met with of success which has seemed to violate the laws of conduct we have evolved. Occasionally we find crime meeting not merely with temporary success, but crowned with a false glory calculated to tempt the weak and to subvert all notions of right and wrong. Occasionally too, we find instances of heroism and virtue overwhelmed with misfortune.

But these instances of criminal success, or of good men suffering unmerited misfortune, need have no effect to weaken our confidence in the rules of conduct herein established. The causes of such success or of such misfortune will always be easily discovered in the ignorance or lack of honesty prevailing among the people in whose midst they occur.

In our own country, when we trace the career of these vicious men, we find their successes, even the most dazzling, to be but ephemeral.

Pursuing their evil courses the more persistently for their success, sooner or later detection and punishment fall upon them ; while the continual dread of detection has, of itself, been a heavy punishment from which they could never set themselves free.

293. Before taking leave of the pupil, it will be well to try and determine some rule or canon by which to recognize good and evil, some measure by which to determine the character of all human acts and conduct. Such a rule can readily be determined by a reference to what has been already learned.

294. Why did we find it to be a good thing that men should be honest and truthful? Why industrious, saving, skillful, sober, obliging and well mannered? It was because these qualities were found to promote the happiness of all, and particularly of the individual practising these virtues.

For the opposite reason we learned it would be evil for men to be idle, to lie, to steal, to cheat, to use false weights and measures, to violate engagements, to live beyond one's means, or even up to them.

295. We found it to be good conduct to sell one's labor, and having sold it, to render it as productivo as possible to the purchaser. Good also to purchase labor, and having purchased it, to direct it to the best advantage, and punctually to pay the price of its hire. We found it to be good conduct to administer capital successfuly, and to lend it to those who could afford to pay the highest rate of interest. We found it to be good conduct to provide good teaching and training for the young, and exceedingly bad conduct to neglect to make such provision.

296. So far as we are able to judge from the accounts given us in books of history, the condition of the world into which the children of to-day have been born is far to be preferred to what that condition was 500, 200, or even 50 years ago.

The buildings, roads, docks, canals, harbors, ships, and telegraphs which minister so wonderfully to our comforts, are the results of a large prevalence of the conduct we have called good. By like conduct these and additional comforts will be preserved and se* cured for future enjoyment, while bad conduct injures and destroys what exists and hinders the production of more.

297. We can now see clearly the rule or canon by which to determine the character of conduct, and what is good and evil. *That is* GOOD *which on a balance of all its consequences tends to promote human happiness*; *and that is* EVIL *which on a like consideration is found to tend to diminish it;* and the goodness or badness of conduct must be tested by its tendency to produce consequences favorable or unfavorable to general well being.

ERATUM.

In chapter X., page 85, the increased or diminished productiveness of the mines has been accidentally omitted from the enumeration of causes which affect the supply and demand of gold and silver.

NOTA BENE.

Since 1868, when the above work was written, so great a change has occurred in the value of silver, owing to the great productiveness of the mines in this country and the demonetization of silver in Germany, that a question which had no significance in 1868 has now become one of importance. The law which established the meaning of the dollar, fixed it at 25.8 grains of standard gold *or* 412½ grains of standard silver. The fall in the value of silver which has happened in consequence of the two causes above named, is just such an accident as is mentioned in chapter X., §155, of which every debtor may by law avail himself, except where otherwise provided by the contract. The fault lay with the ignorance of the people and of the Congress of 1837, in giving the name "dollar" to two distinct things.

APPENDIX.

Review Questions.

The following questions will enable the teacher to use this book as a catechetical class book ; or as a reading book to be reviewed by aid of the questions. They will also aid students who have not the assistance of a teacher to ascertain when they have mastered the meaning of the text.

In any case additional questions should be introduced either by the teacher to stimulate the interest of his class, or by the student to exercise his ingenuity, and to place the subject before himself from different points of view.

The questions may however be followed literally, and still cover the text in most cases.

The author urges upon teachers to multiply appropriate questions, and with this view, these questions are designed to be suggestive as well as direct.

He also recommends students who have not the assistance of a teacher, but who are desirous of acquiring the all-important knowledge attempted to be placed before them in this book, and which they have not had the opportunity of acquiring at school, to form themselves into classes and to meet at each other's houses, or other convenient places, to catechize one another and discuss the subjects of the book. Chiefly to facilitate such exercises the black figures, (referring to the numbered paragraphs in the text,) are placed over the questions relating thereto.

CHAPTER I.

1.

. 1. Name some of the comforts enjoyed by children in the United States.

2. Have you given much thought to the labor required to be performed to supply you with those comforts? If not, why not?

4—12.

4. Give the history of a woolen stocking, of a cotton shirt, of a stove, of a locomotive, of a plough, of a loaf of bread, of a loom, of a sewing machine, of a cup of cocoa, coffee or tea, etc., etc.

13.

5. What is a plough? A spinning machine? A carding machine? A spade? A pair of scissors? A sewing machine?

6. What do men plough? What do men dig? When do men plough rather than dig, and when do they dig rather than plough? What do men spin? card? weave? What, with what, how, and why do men plough, dig, spin, card, weave, quarry, build, mine, forge, bake, boil, brew, cut, sew, fit, wash, write, print and publish?

14.

7. What name is given to include all the necessaries and comforts of life produced by labor?

8. Define wealth.

Note.—This first chapter is a very important one, and too much pains cannot be bestowed upon its elucidation until the pupils have thoroughly mastered it.

The younger the pupils the more objectively and fully the subjects referred to should be treated.

Models or drawings of the industrial implements spoken of and of any others which may suggest themselves to the teacher should be procured or made, and the interest of the pupils awakened and kept alive by presenting in new and varied aspects the objects common to their every day life.

CHAPTER II.

18.

9. Are all the necessaries of life wealth? If not, name those which are not.

19—21.

11. Are earth, water, or air ever wealth? If they are, state when and where.

22.

12. What does labor create?

13. What does labor do? And illustrate your answer.

23.

14. What is a commodity?

24.

15. What kind of people produced the wealth we find now in existence?

16. Do all persons labor?

17. What relation exists between the proportion of the non-workers to the workers, and the amount of wealth produced?

25.

18. How may the young become able and willing to labor.

2

19. What name is given to those who labor cheerfully and continuously?

20. Define Industry.

29.

21. What do we live upon while tilling the ground, and sowing the seed?

22. What did the men who produced what we are now consuming live upon while laboring to produce?

30.

23. Explain the chief distinction between the savage and civilized man.

33.

24. How many principal harvests are there in a year in most countries?

25. How many appetites have you each day? How many in the year?

26. How shall one harvest be made to satisfy 3×365 or 1095 appetites?

27. Are harvests always abundant?

28. How can the abundance of one harvest be made to supply the scarcity of another?

29. If the principle food of a people cannot be saved from one year to another could any provision be made against scarcity, and how?

30. What kind of people are they likely to be who rely mainly on one perishable article for food?

31. Would they be likely to make such provision as is necessary, and if not, why not?

32. Contrast corn, wheat, rye, or rice with potatoes, and state what kind of people would be likely to use corn, wheat, rye, or rice, as their staple article of food, and what kind of people would rely upon potatoes, and give your reasons in each case.

35.

33. What do aqueducts, ships, docks, piers, canals, railroads, etc., teach us with regard to saving in the past; and how?

36.

34. What name is given to the quality of saving?
35. Is saving necessary in the future, and why?

40.

36. What is skill?
37. What is knowledge?
38. Are skill and knowledge desirable, and why?

45.

39. Name and define afresh, the four conditions of human well-being examined in this chapter.

NOTE.—Although the answers to questions numbered 29 to 32 are not directly furnished in the text, the deductions are so easy that the teacher will find no difficulty in leading his class *to find out for themselves* the truth on the matters referred to by the Socratic process of leading the pupil by questions from one truth to another less obvious than the first. He will at the same time be training his pupils to *think*, and to think logically.

CHAPTER III.
46.
40. What is Division of labor?
47.
41. Show how it affects the efficiency of labor.

42. Give Adam Smith's illustration of the advantages of division of labor.
48.
43. Does the carpenter co-operate with the farmer to produce grain, and how? Does the tailor co-operate with the potter to produce earthenware, and how?

44. Give various instances of the co-operation of one kind of workman with another.
49.
45. Do those engaged in household labors co-operate to produce grain, ships, bridges, railroads, etc., and how?
50.
46. What has tended to throw household labors chiefly into the hands of women in this country?
51.
47. For what other vocation do women seem to be specially adapted, and why?

CHAPTER IV.
53.
48. What new duty is thrown upon the laborer by division of labor?

55.

49. On what will depend the quantity of commodities he will be able to procure?

. 56.

50. Does this bring into view any and what harmony of industry?

51. Explain the consequences which would follow if man were so constituted as to seek the happiness of others without regard to his own.

CHAPTER V.

59.

52. Why does man labor?

53. What would be the result of depriving him of what he had labored to produce?

61.

54. How might protection to property be certainly and perfectly secured?

62.

55. Why are taxes raised?

63.

56. Out of what are taxes paid?

57. What effect has the paying of taxes on the inducement to labor and save?

64.

58. What further difficulty exists in the way of affording protection to property?

65.

59. What is the most efficient police?

66.

60. Contrast the order of the scientific evolution of honesty as a condition of human well-being, with its proper place in teaching and training, and give reasons for the place you assign to it.

67.

61. How is society further injured by dishonesty?

69.

62. What is the limit to the power of the best of governments in regard to wealth?

71.

63. Name some indirect consequences to society from dishonesty.

NOTE.—The teacher should not quit this chapter without giving his pupils numerous illustrations both of honesty and dishonesty.

The importance of truthfulness, the happiness existing in a community in which it prevails, the discomfort which attends its violation both in the case of individuals and of society, using illustrations to bring home to the conscience of every child the nature of true honor contrasted with its sham, should be minutely dwelt upon and profusely illustrated.

The care taken of the property of others, both public and private, as, for instance, of the school furniture, etc., will gauge pretty accurately the moral status of the scholars.

The demoralization produced by examples of dishonesty, especially when successful, should also be pointed out.

The consequences produced by national dishonesty in the

transfer of capital from the country where the dishonesty prevails, or the hindering its flow to such a country from others,
should only be slighty touched upon with very young pupils,
but should be dwelt upon with older students.

———

CHAPTER VI.

75.

64. How may the wealthless obtain a share of wealth to supply
their immediate wants?

76.

65. Who have the enjoyment of the wealth employed in the
purchase of the right to the future product of labor?

77.

66. Define wages and capital.

78—9—80.

67. Are capitalists and laborers distinct persons? Give illustrations to prove your answer.

68. What is interest?

82.

69. What regulates the average rate of wages? Prove your
answer.

84—5.

70. How are individual wages regulated?

71. Do high wages paid to one workmen diminish the wages
paid to others? If not, why not?

72. What advantage has an inferior workman in being placed under a trustworthy foreman?

87.

73. How may increased wages be obtained?

88.

74. To what are wages proportioned?

75. What effect has such proportionment on general conduct?

89.

76. Name some of the circumstances affecting the wages paid in different trades.

90.

77. What should determine in this country the selection of a trade and of an employer, in the case of young persons about to learn a trade.

91.

78. How may a good workman free himself from a bad employer?

92—3.

79. To what should workmen look as the cause of insufficiency in their wages, and how should they set about obtaining good wages?

CHAPTER VII.

94.

80. What induces the owner of wealth to employ it as capital?

81. What is profit?

82. Is profit certain? Prove your answer.

95.

83. Analyse profit.

96.

84. What is the tendency of the rate of profit in different trades?

97.

85. Name some of the qualifications of a successful capitalist.

98.

86. Who, if any one, is benefitted besides the capitalist by the profit he realizes? Prove your answer.

99.

87. Are the interests of capitalist and laborer antagonistic or coincident? Prove your answer.

100.

88. What is labor's best friend, and why?

CHAPTER VIII.

101—6.

89. Ought property in land to be recognized?
90. Why or why not?

107—8.

91. What is rent?
92. How does it arise?
93. Is the amount of rent always the same, and if not, what determines its variations?

9

94. What considerations influence the amount of rent a tenant may be willing to pay? •

109—10—11.

95. Illustrate differences in and growth of rent.

112.

96. Is rent a cause of dearness?

97. Is it a result of comparative difficulty of production?

98. Prove your answer.

99. Under what circumstances is rent a fitting subject for taxation?

113.

100. What is the effect of competition among tenants?

114.

. 101. What is the difference between Europe and America with regard to the growth of rent?

115.

102. What lesson is taught by the contrast, and how?
    •

116.   ·

103. What common belief is now seen to be an error?

CHAPTER IX.

117—118.

104. What is value?

119 –120.

105. What is "intrinsic" value?

121.

106. How is value determined and measured? Give different illustrations in support of your answer.

127—132.

107. What is market value, and how is it regulated? Illustrate your answer.

133.

108. What services are rendered by the successful speculator?

134.

109. What is meant by 'the equation of supply and demand'?

135—6.

110. What is average value? How is it regulated?

137.

111. What are essential to the possession of value by any com-. modity?

NOTE.—Care should be taken to clear up the prevailing ambiguity in the use of the words "value" and "intrinsic value."

The topic should not be left until the pupils have thoroughly clear ideas on the subject of value, and how it is measured and determined.

The pupil should be required to suggest illustrations of the principles established in the text.

Teacher and pupils alike will readily perceive that the questions to this chapter, as to many of the others, are skeletons merely, to be filled out by them with numerous other questions suggested by the text, as well as by questions which will be suggested by the pupils' answers.

Self-students will find a good practice in framing fresh questions to themselves.

CHAPTER X.

138-39-40.

112. What were the most important means adopted to facilitate interchange?

141.

113. What purposes are served by standards of measure, and how?

114. How may the full advantages to bo obtained from them be secured ?

143.

˙What name is given to the measure of value?

144-145.

115. What is essential to a measure of length? To a measure of value ?

146.

116. What had to be specially provided against in the selection of the standard measure of value?

147.

117. What consideration mainly led to the selection of gold or silver as the material out of which to construct the measure of value?

148—51.

118. Name the qualities which specially adapt gold and silver for that purpose.

119. Do gold and silver fluctuate in value?

120. Where would you look for the cause of fluctuations in the value of gold as measured, (say) in iron rails, and why ?

152.

121. Name the causes which affect the value of gold and silver.

153.

122. What would be the effect of an increase in the quantity of gold in any community upon the quantity of other commodities?

154—156.

123. Give an illustration of the difference between reduced currency, and a debased currency.

NOTE.—The questions to Chapter X., as indeed to most of the chapters, are meant as indications only of the questions which the text suggests.

The teacher or self-student should supply many more, until certain that the subject is thoroughly mastered.

CHAPTER XI.

157.

124. What is price?

158—9.

125. Describe the progress and effect of a rise in price in the case of any particular commodity?

126. Is a rise in price a bad thing?

127. If not, does it denote the existence of any, and of what evil?

128. When the evil exists or is threatened, is the rise in price a good or bad thing, and why?

160.

129. What function is performed by the speculator?

161.

130. Is there a conflict or harmony of interests between the speculator and the community in which his operations are conducted?

131. What effect has this conflict or harmony on the skill, knowledge, and judgment of those engaged in commerce?

162.

132. Are the prices of commodities higher in the country from or to which they are exported?

133. What is the effect of the exportation of gold or silver?

CHAPTER XII.

163.

134. What thought should be in the mind both of capitalist and laborer?

164.

135. What is a certain means by which profits and wages may .be increased?

166.

136. What is meant by a combination?

167.

137. Is any agreement needed to induce people to do what they think is for their interest?

138. Ought they to agree to do what is for their injury?

168.

139. How can laborers induce capitalists to convert wealth into capital?

140. What would be the effect upon the profits of capitalists of a rise in wages without any increase in its productiveness?

141. Would capitalists be induced thereby to increase or diminish the capital employed by them?

142. Is then a rise in the wages of all laborers possible otherwise than by increasing the productiveness of their labor?

143. Trace the effects of a combination to raise wages in some particular trade.

169—170.

144. What is a strike?

145. Describe its effect?

171.

146. What serves to conceal the effects of a strike?

172.

147. Give an illustration of the loss resulting from a strike to those engaged in it.

173.

148. Who may be made more wealthy by a strike?

149. Who, besides those who make it, are injured by a strike?

150. Show how long it would take to make up the loss occasioned by an apparently successful strike.

174.

151. What would be the effect of a strike entered into to procure a reduction in the hours of labor?

175.

152. How might the hours of labor of the workers be advantageously reduced?

176.

153. Give an illustration in support of your answer to the last question.

177.

154. Describe the conduct which has been pursued by Trades Unions.

(1.) With regard to the savings of its members.

(2.) With regard to rendering labor more productive, or the reverse.

179.

155. For what purpose are capitalists likely to combine? Describe the probable effects of such a combination.

180—81.

156. What is co-operation?

157. Who co-operate?

182.

158. What is meant by a "Co-operative" shop?

159. What advantages, (if any,) does it present over other shops?

160. What is the chief difficulty in the way of securing those advantages?

183.

161. Give some account of the most successful efforts to secure those advantages.

162. What was the conduct of a Trades Union towards one of them?

163. What shall be said of the workmen who submitted to the Trades Union in that instance?

164. What shall be said of workmen who submit to the tyranny of Trades Unions in other cases?

184.

165. What is a "Co-operative store?" What is the real nature of the payment made to the customers at such stores under the name of dividend?

185.

166. To what has the success of "co-operative" stores and shops been chiefly owing.

188.

167. To which of the elements of profit does the large profit made by successful "co-operative" stores chiefly belong?

168. How does the society become the owners of such profit?

NOTE.—No amount of time will be too great to devote to the subject of this chapter.

The history of many strikes should be obtained and communicated to the class. The rules of different trades unions, and especially their secret proceedings and traditional practices, which they take care to keep out of their books of rules, should be ascertained and laid before the pupils, who should be led *by the Socratic method of teaching* to observe for themselves their pernicious character.

The beneficial effects of giving the employés an interest in the future result of their labors should be dwelt upon, but at the same time the fact should be made clear that, though the reward to labor may be thereby increased, it is only by the increased

9*

value of the product of their labor, and not by the defeating of any occult manœuvres of hostile employers, that this result is secured.

•

CHAPTER XIII.

188—9.

169. By what means can the labor of interchange be further diminished?

170. What is credit?

190.

171. How can the full benefits of credit be realized?

172. Who is relieved from all difficulty as to fulfilling his engagements?

173. Ought credit to be taken for purposes of unproductive consumption, and if not, why not?

191.

174. Give an illustration of the benefits resulting from a judicious use of credit.

175. Describe the precautions to be taken both in taking and giving credit.

192.

176. Is one who does not take credit under any obligation as to the persons to whom he gives credit? Give reasons for your answer.

193.

177. What is the effect of laws purporting to aid in the compulsory recovery of debts?

CHAPTER XIV.

194.

178. By whom are Bills of Exchange said to have been invented?

179. Was their invention a benefit, and why?

195.

180. What is a Bill of Exchange?

196.

181. Illustrate its use.

182. What names are given to the various parties to a bill of exchange and to those into whose hands it passes?

183. What is a foreign bill of Exchange?

184. What is an inland bill?

197.

185. Between what places are the advantages of the use of bills of exchange greatest?

186. Describe the effects of a lack of probity or punctuality in the use of bills.

198.

187. What are Post Office money orders?

199.

188. What is a promissory note?

200.

189. What is the limit to the value of a bill or note discounted at the place where it is made payable?

190. What is the limit to the value of a bill or note drawn in a place distant from that where it is sold or discounted?

191. What is the rate of exchange ?

192. When is the rate of exchange at par?

193. Suppose New York to owe more money to London, Paris and Hamburg, than those cities owe to New York, will bills on those places be above or below par?

201.

194. How is the par of exchange between two countries which have the same commodity as a measure of value ascertained?

195. What is the par between the United States gold currency and that of England ?

202.

196. Ascertain the par of exchange between the United States debased paper currency, at various rates of its debasement, and the currencies of Great Britain, France and Germany respectively?

203.

197. Describe the complication introduced into the exchanges between this country and Great Britain?

NOTE.—The teacher should take the opportunity afforded by § 194 to combat the prejudices which he will probably find some of his pupils will have imbibed against the Jews. He might make himself acquainted with some of the bitter cruelties and persecutions to which they were subjected by the peoples of Europe through the ignorance and superstition of the latter ; while the degraded condition of Spain will furnish a striking illustration of the natural punishment of such crimes.

He should collect instances of the grand features in the character of this remarkable race (the Jews), and particularly of their trustworthiness and probity ; the facts regarding them proving that, in complete opposition to the prevailing prejudices. they are far superior in honesty and general trustworthiness, *wherever they are trusted*, to the generality of other races.

CHAPTER XV.`

205.

198. Describe the primary function of a banker?

199. What is the commodity in which the banker deals?

206.

200. Describe the mode of doing business with regard to (1) drawing accounts and (2) deposit accounts?

207.

201. Describe the difference between a banker as the debtor of his customers and other debtors?

208—9—10.

202. Describe the operation and effect of the discounting of commercial bills by bankers?

211—12.

203. What is the Clearing House?

204. Describe its advantages as regards economizing labor, and the amount of money each banker would, but for the Clearing House, have to keep on hand?

213—14.

205. Give some account of the New York Clearing House?

215—16.

206. What unexpected advantages have accrued from the establishment of the New York Clearing House ?

219.

207. What are the principal objections to the National Bank Act ?

220.

208. What are savings banks ?
209. What is the nature of their accounts ?
210. What rules should govern their management, and why ?

221.

211. What are some of the special advantages furnished by savings banks ?
212. What should be the most important consideration with depositors at those banks ?

CHAPTER XVL.

223.

213. What is interest ?

224.

214. What is it persons really desire to borrow when they ask for a loan ?
215. Name some errors common with persons who speak of money and interest?

225.

216. What determines the market rate of interest ?   [Demand

and supply.]
217. What limits the market rate of interest?

226.

218. What limits the average rate of interest?

227—8.

219. Explain the tendency of labor and capital to flow to this country from Europe, and how this tendency may be checked.

220. What is the effect of competition among capitalists for the capital coming from Europe upon the wages of labor, and the administration of capital?

229.

221. What is the effect of usury laws?

230.

222. Analyze interest and point out the elements which are most liable to fluctnations.

CHAPTER XVII.

231—2.

223. What is paper money?

233.

224. With what kind of paper money is the name generally associated?

234.

225. What is a dollar?

226. What is the promise made by the maker of a note or bill which specifies a promise to pay a given number of dollars?

227. Is the promise performed by giving for it another promise?

228. What is the character of men who refuse to fulfill their promises, but offer instead only another promise?

235—6.

229. How can confidence in the performance of promises be established?

230. If you were quite sure that the promise on a bill to pay a given number of dollars would be performed on request, which would you rather have to carry about with you, a bill promising to pay one thousand dollars, or one thousand dollars in gold or silver?

231. If you would rather have the promise than the metal, what do you think other people would generally desire, and why?

237.

232. How could more promises to pay be made to circulate than people required?

238.

233. What is an inconvertible paper money?

239.

234. What must be said of the intelligence and honesty of a people among whom an inconvertible paper currency prevails?

240.

235. Who are the greatest sufferers by a depreciated currency?

241—3.

236. Did the forcing an inconvertible currency upon the peo-

ple of the United States give additional resources to the government for the prosecution of the civil war? ˌ

237. Describe its actual effect.

244.

238. Show how the history of the depreciation of the currency of the United States illustrates the truth of your answer to the last question.

245, 6—7.

239. Describe the commercial condition attending a progressive depreciation of the currency, and of attempts to return to honest dealing.

248.

240. Of what does the currency of the United States consist irrespective of commercial credits?

249.

241. Contrast the course adopted by the French since the Franco-Prussian war with ours, since our civil war.

250.

242. What regulations should government prescribe for the conduct of the business of baking?

243. What regulations should government prescribe for the conduct of the business of banking?

CHAPTER XVIII.

251.

244. What is a crisis?

245. What is a panic?

246. What would render commercial crises and panics impossible ?

252.

247. Describe the cause and effects of a general state of commercial mistrust.

253.

248. What conduct should be pursued by laborers to protect themselves from suffering through displacement occasioned by commercial failures ?

254--6.

249. Describe the rise and progress of a commercial crisis ?

257.

250. How may unwise legislation convert a crisis into a panic ?

258.

251. What is the cause of a crisis ?

259.

252. Describe the effect upon the currency of the destruct of credit ?

253. How does credit postpone a demand for money ?

260—1.

254. Point out how the evils of legislative interference are most felt in times of commercial mistrust ?

262.

255. How may commercirl crises and panics be prevented ?

CHAPTER XIX.

263.

256. So far as yet examined, what have we found to be the effect of legislative interference with commerce ?

264—5.

257. What is foreign commerce ?
258. How has foreign commerce arisen ?

266.

259. What conflict has been found between the commercial interests of any one part of the world with those of any other ?
260. What harmony has been apparent ?

267.

261. By whom and how has the such harmony been interfered with ?
262. Could such interference be justifiable under any circumstances ?

268—9.

263. What question is involved in every proposal to impose a tariff on foreign produce ?

270.

264. What would seem to be a more logical course of proceeding ?
265. What do the directors of labor and capital do when not interfered with ?
266. Ought legislators to interfere with their so doing, and if not, why not ?

212 of political economy.

212 FIRST STEPS IN POLITICAL ECONOMY.

212 FIRST STEPS IN POLITICAL ECONOMY.

271.

267. What determines the nature of the trade between different places ?

272.

268. What would naturally be the articles generally produced (1) in densely peopled countries ; (2) in less thickly peopled countries, the state of civilization being supposed equal ?

269. Does government protect the producer in the enjoyment of what he has produced by imposing restraints upon his liberty to exchange his products for anything else he desires ?

273.

270. How has the cry, "Protection to native industry," arisen ?

274.

271. What is pauper labor ?

272. What is likely to have been the object of persons using that expression ?

275.

273. How has the farmer been "protected" by preventing him from exchanging his corn for iron from England, Sweden or Sardinia ?

274. Why could not the American iron-master compete with the English or Swedish ?

276.

275. What is a pauper ?

276. On whose industry do the laborers of Europe subsist ?

277. On whose industry do the iron-masters of Pennsylvania and cotton spinners of Lowell subsist, at least in part ?

278. Do they themselves assert that their own labor is not sufficiently productive to support them ?   Prove your answer.

279. Who, then, are paupers ?

277.

280. Can it be true that the civilized farmer of the United States cannot " *compete*" with the Boers or Kaffirs of Africa ?

281. What is a competing man ?

282. What advantage do Europe and America gain in exchanging their products for the wool raised by the Boer or Kaffir ?

283. What advantage does the Boer or Kaffir get by the exchange ?

278.

284. Does the imposition of a tariff increase or diminish the burthen of taxation ?

279.

285. Can any and what part of the duty on imported goods be thrown upon the people of the country exporting them ?

286. When, by reason of the duty, goods cease to be imported, what is the effect upon the people ? Upon those who produce the taxed commodity ?

287. In which case would the loss to the people be less ; (1.) to continue the tax whereby the importation is prevented, or (2.) to raise by direct taxation a sum, equal to the rate of duty multiplied by the entire amount consumed, and to hand that sum over directly to those engaged in producing the taxed commodtiy on condition that they never did another stroke of work so long as the like payment continued to be yearly made to them ?

280.

288. What particular anomaly is presented in the cry for " protection " on account of the heavy taxes paid by the people of the United States ?

281.

289. Can the fact that wages, rents, and taxes are lower among

other nations than with us render customs duties desirable to "protect" our industry? If not, why not?

282.

290. Is any additional source of employment obtained for labor by any amount of customs duties? If not, why not?

283.

291. Name some of the moral objections to a Tariff.

284—8.

292. Give some illustrations from the business of assaying and mining of the effects of customs duties in diminishing the employment for and the productiveness of labor.

293. Give illustrations from any other trades.

294. What has been the effect of the Tariff on the real wages of skilled laborers in this country?

295. What has been its effect on unskilled labor?

296. What effect is it likely to have on the class of persons immigrating to this country?

289—90.

297. What relation existed between the British corn laws and the Irish famine of 1846-7.

CHAPTER XX.

291.

298. Has the student of the foregoing pages learned all that is known of the science of human well-being?

292.

299. What has he learned?

293.

300. What apparent exceptions will he meet with to the laws he has examined?

301. Should such exceptions discourage him, and if not, why not?

302. Where may he expect to find the cause of undeserved success or of unmerited misfortune?

294—5.

303. What acts have been found to be good, and what evil, and why?

296.

304. How come we to be better off to-day than our predecessors?

297.

305. How may we provide that our successors shall be yet better provided for than we are?

298.

306. Lay down a canon for determining GOOD and EVIL.

307. How shall the goodness or badness of conduct be determined?

NEW BOOKS.

EVOLUTION AND PROGRESS:
By Rev. Wm. I. Gill, A. M...................... ᴾrice $1 50
ANALYTICAL PROCESSES:
By Rev. Wm. I. Gill, A. M.................. " 2 00
ECCLESIOLOGY:
By Rev. E. J. Fish, D. D................. " 2 00
GOLD AND FREE BANKS:
By M. R. Pilon............................. " 0 75
THE MANUSCRIPT MANUAL: ·
An Aid to Authors......... .... " 0 10
IRENE; or, BEACH-BROKEN BIL-
LOWS:
By Mrs. B. F. Baer......................... " 1 25
WILD FLOWERS. Poems:
By C. W. Hubner........................... " 1 25
HER WAITING HEART:
By Lou. Capsadell.......................... " 1 25
SHADOWED PERILS:
By M. A. Avery............................. " 1 25
WOMEN'S SECRETS; or, HOW
TO BE BEAUTIFUL:
By Lou. Capsadell.......................... " 0 75
EGYPT ENNIS; or, PRISONS
WITHOUT WALLS.
By Kelsie Etheridge........................ " 0 50
THE TRAVELERS' GRAB BAG:
By an Old Traveler......................... " 0 50
NINE LITTLE BUSTERS:
By Kelsie Etheridge........................ " 0 25

Inclose three-cent stamp for pamphlet, comprising dedescriptive catalogue, and the plan of organization and working of The Authors' Publishing Company. Address

THE AUTHORS' PUBLISHING CO.,

27 *BOND ST., NEW YORK.*

www.ingramcontent.com/pod-product-compliance
Lightning Source LLC
Chambersburg PA
CBHW030821270326
41928CB00007B/829